TO BE A SOLDIER

TO BE A SOLDIER

Joining the British Army

RICHARD O'CONNOR

Airlife
England

Copyright © 1996 Richard O'Connor

First published in the UK in 1996
by Airlife Publishing Ltd

British Library Cataloguing in Publication Data
  A catalogue record for this book
  is available from the British Library

ISBN 1 85310 750 6

Typeset by Hewer Text Composition Services, Edinburgh
Printed in England by Livesey Ltd., Shrewsbury

Airlife Publishing Ltd
101 Longden Road, Shrewsbury, SY3 9EB, England.

Acknowledgments

During the two years it has taken me to research and write this book, I have received help from more people than I could hope to mention individually. The Ministry of Defence has been very co-operative, and has allowed me unlimited access to many training establishments and regiments. I would particularly like to thank Brigadier (now Major-General) Chris Elliott, Director of Army Recruiting, and Major Tim Grant, Royal Artillery.

I am very grateful to all the public relations staff at the Ministry of Defence, who arranged many visits to regiments in this country and abroad. I must also thank the Army Careers Information Offices in Birmingham, Warwick and Coventry, Lieutenant-Colonel R N B Quicke, Light Infantry, the Army Training Regiments at Winchester and Lichfield, and the Royal Armoured Corps Trade Training Depot in Bovington, Dorset.

My thanks also go to the following commanding officers, who provided much assistance and information: Lieutenant-Colonel S R B Allen, The Royal Scots Dragoon Guards; Lieutenant-Colonel N J Hall, The Duke of Wellington's Regiment; Lieutenant-Colonel A J Whistler, 2nd Bn Royal Regiment of Fusiliers; Lieutenant-Colonel C M Eastland, Royal Signals; and all those officers in many units and establishments who made my visits so enjoyable.

I must also mention those soldiers and civilians whom I asked to read and comment on individual chapters of the book, in particular Colonel J Smith, Royal Artillery, and Mr Steven Boag, but above all my girlfriend Kim, who put up with my many weeks away, and my editor Charles Heyman. Their comments on the manuscript have been of incalculable help.

My greatest thanks, though, must go to the many anonymous commissioned and non-commissioned officers who agreed to be interviewed. Without their time, honesty, frankness and above all their sense of humour, this book would never have been possible.

Contents

Introduction

The relationship between the British public and the Army has always been one of distant affection, with few civilians knowing much about the reality of service life. This book is an attempt to bridge the gap and to explain how today's Army works, its strengths and its weaknesses. It explores how today's modern soldiers are recruited and trained, their behaviour and their lives.

The idea for this book was first put to me long before I left the Army. With many regiments suffering a shortage of manpower and the standard of new recruits considered by those training them to be below what was required, there was a need for a book about joining the Army written by someone with recent military experience but far enough removed to provide an independent view. The book does not set out to promote the Army as a career; in fact, some might say it is the opposite.

This seems the most appropriate time to present it. With falling recruitment figures and increasing resignations the Army is facing a time of extreme pressure. Manpower has always presented it with its most persistent problem. Bad recruitment years are followed by good ones, and the Army has been able to maintain a bumpy balance, but its difficulties are likely to increase in the next few years, mainly because many soldiers feel they are underpaid and overworked. The Army has shrunk but its horizons and commitments have widened. Nevertheless, although some famous old regiments have been forced into shotgun marriages, the Army as a whole has emerged with its reputation enhanced rather than diminished and even the worst-affected branch, the infantry, has maintained and even improved its highly professional image.

Many of today's soldiers can still be identified with those of the past: they are loyal, disciplined, rarely snobbish, but often vain. And whether on ceremonial duties in London or patrolling the streets of Northern Ireland, the British

1

Army still remains the most respected of all the world's fighting forces.

In the forthcoming years, contrary to what is reported in the media, an extra 15,000 recruits will be required to fill its ranks and to replace those soldiers who will retire. Never before have there been such opportunities for those looking for a worthwhile and rewarding career. In the words of one senior commanding officer, 'If ever there was a time to join the Army, it is now.'

To make the book more accessible to the outsider, I have tried to use the minimum of military terms and acronyms, but in the interests of accuracy I have not been able to avoid them entirely. There is an alphabetical guide to army jargon and slang at the end of the book.

I hope I have succeeded in providing an insight into how the new generation of soldiers are recruited and trained. In order to achieve this, the book follows every stage of the selection process for both private soldiers and the officer cadets. It moves from recruitment to basic training, through to trade training and on to the soldiers' first months with their new regiments; including the daily routine, nights on the town, girlfriends, and the media myths of racism and bullying. It looks at the turmoils of marriage and the joy of promotion, and ends with the most difficult question of all, the Army's future.

CHAPTER 1

Joining the Army

'A *Soldier*! – a common *Soldier*! – nothing but
a body that makes movements when it hears
a shout.'

D H Lawrence, 1913

Amongst the asphalt walkways and concrete ramps of the Palisades Shopping Centre in the heart of Birmingham curious shoppers stop briefly to peer into the windows. In one, however, there is no ordinary merchandise on sale. A large model battleship sits proudly in its glass case in the centre of the Army and Navy Careers Information Office, surrounded by posters of tanks speeding into combat and fusiliers over-running enemy positions. A buzzer sounds on the door and a recruiting sergeant lifts his head from the paperwork that fills his tray and acknowledges an applicant. With the threat of terrorist attacks on 'soft' targets, military commanders are not prepared to take any risks and have installed security equipment that would not look out of place in a top jewellers. The sergeant's hand drops and releases the electronic door catch and the applicant steps into a world where rank and red tape rule.

There has always been a need for a selection process to find those applicants who have a high degree of intelligence and who are quick on the uptake, yet the cost, in both time and hard cash, has always been considered excessive by Ministry of Defence (MoD) officials. One officer said, 'We live in a world where modern warfare has become a more technical, push-button existence . . . the Army still needs to find high-calibre recruits . . . but nowadays the resources are not there to sustain the long recruitment procedures we currently have; an applicant can be waiting in excess of eighteen months for a place.'

The future of the Army's recruitment and selection pro-gramme came under review in the Front Line First initiative.

This review found that recruitment cost some £100m annually, with each recruit's enlistment accounting for between £5,000 and £15,000, depending on the regiment or corps. With the Government's jittery budget masters intent on cutting costs, the recommendation that all the Careers Offices be closed came as no surprise. A pilot project currently under way at selected Job Centres is the first stage of the programme, with Job Centres advertising for recruits. This serves to provide the Army with a much larger shop window than they once had, but Army Careers Information Offices are nevertheless likely to remain open for some time.

These changes are sure to reassure those teenagers and adults who find the thought of stepping into the Army Careers Information Office, and being faced with the six-foot 'barn-door' recruitment sergeant, too daunting. That two-thirds of today's adult population have at some time in their lives thought about joining the armed forces, but over half have never gone any further, is a testament to that feeling of intimidation.

The British Army has battled to fill its ranks since National Service ended, and at no time have recruiting officers been able to sit back and take it easy. In the last 20 years the recruitment pattern has been one of peaks and troughs. During the peak periods, which normally arise during a time of national crisis like the Falklands Campaign and the Gulf War, the Director of Army Recruiting in London has been able to smile and look forward to a healthy intake, but in the trough periods, like that of the mid-eighties, he has had to hold his breath and hope.

The defence cuts in 1991 have also resulted in poor recruitment figures and yet another trough, with a 35 per cent decline in applications. Confidence in the military as a career has been seriously eroded; with the sweeping redundancy programme, many members of the public now assume that the Army no longer needs to recruit. Only time will tell if it is able to follow this trough with a peak, but it is more likely as Job Centres start to promote the Army, and recruitment figures should then increase rather than decrease in the long term.

The biggest challenge the Army has to face in a changing world is to give itself a new and interesting image. During peak periods it can afford to boast in its advertisements, 'Are you good enough for the Regular Army?', but in trough periods it has to advertise more of the attractions of the jobs, such as promotion, pay and the exciting life.

In the past the Army has been criticised for its advertising campaigns, with many people feeling they give a glamourised and unrealistic view of military life and fail to point out the disadvantages. This is almost certainly true, and many serving soldiers shake their heads and whisper obscenities when the adverts appear. But to expect the Director of Army Recruiting at the MoD to paint a more accurate picture of service life would, in today's climate, be wishful thinking.

Television and cinema advertising is only the tip of the iceberg in a massive public relations campaign. Today the Army uses both local and national promotional activities, and maximises Keeping the Army in the Public Eye (KAPE) teams, with their light tracked combat vehicles, who set up demonstration stands in city centres and hand out regimental leaflets to bump up local recruitment. Opportunities like the Royal Tournament and assistance to the *Soldier, Soldier* television programme all serve their purpose, and help fill the recruiting offices and entice the young.

Whatever promotional activity is used to spark the initial interest, when applicants actually enter recruiting offices, it is usually because of a national campaign rather than the strength of any local regiment; a surprising nine out of ten applicants have no specific regiment in mind.

Whatever the final regiment chosen, there are many mixed reasons why young men and women join today's modern Army. In a society where the pursuit of prosperity and success are uppermost in the minds of young people and where the Army does little to dispel rising public fears about its well-publicised redundancy programme, it is not surprising that few are turning to the Army for a career; those that do are often fleeing broken homes and growing dole queues. The Army has historically been the 'parent' of young people escaping domestic violence, abuse and crime-riddled inner cities.

Many recruits crave the excitement, adventure and sense of belonging the Army can give. While many applicants want to join in order to build confidence and gain respect, the more mature and wiser ones often want to learn a trade, gain qualifications and move up the promotion ladder. Some also join to mature, to gain experience and to use the

Army as a stepping-stone to acquire skills to take back into civilian life.

Very few applicants, apart from those who come from service families or the Cadet Forces, are likely to know what Army life is really like. One recruitment officer said, 'It is deeply disturbing that today's youth are totally out of touch with the realities of Army life.' But he also admitted the irony that little is done to change their view.

The Army has realised these potential problems, and training regiments are now more flexible in dealing with mismatched recruits and try to find them alternative trades. With a recruiting cost in excess of £7,000, this proves to be a cheaper and more effective answer than simply letting the recruit leave.

Joining Up

All enlistments start with a short visit to the local Army Careers Information Office. A recruiting sergeant will begin by ensuring that the applicant meets the basic criteria to join. Applicants must have British, Commonwealth or Republic of Ireland citizenship and must be aged 16 for junior soldiers and over $17\frac{1}{2}$ for adult service. The upper age limit is 25, although there are higher limits for specialist professions such as trained nurses, radiographers and physiotherapists, who may enter up to the age of 33 years, and solicitors and ordained clergy up to the age of 45 years. Candidates must have no serious crimes to their name; this is checked by the Army's Manning and Records Office via a link to Scotland Yard's National Criminal Records File. Many enlistments have been refused entry at a late stage of training for not declaring fines or court appearances. Such offences by no means exclude the applicant, but acceptance depends on their severity; the Rehabilitation of Offenders Act 1975 also stops any person on probation from joining.

There are no longer service engagements where applicants sign on for three, six, or nine years. All soldiers are enlisted on an open engagement, which is for a period of 22 years' service from the age of 18 or the date of entry, whichever is later. All soldiers have the right to leave after the completion of three years' service from the age of 18 and one year's notice is required. The only exception to this is in the case of pregnancy, when women may choose either to resign or take maternity leave; the latter option is the most widely taken.

The recruiting sergeant will go through the applicants' schooling, qualifications, employment and family circumstances, and will check whether the applicant has any preferences for possible regiments or corps. He will then explain what life in the Army is like and the work the recruit will do. The applicant will be given pamphlets on local regiments and told to go home and think about it. When a firm application is made, the candidate will be given an 'application to enlist' and 'medical questionnaire' form to fill in and a date will be arranged for educational tests.

Educational Tests

The Army needs men and women who can master and control the high-powered technology of today's modern weapons equipment and information, so the selection programme requires all applicants take a set of basic educational tests. With over 130 jobs and trades to choose from, the selection staff need to know the intellectual capacity of the potential recruit. There are some jobs which they have no problems in filling, and others where the difficulty is acute. The attraction of acquiring a heavy goods vehicle driving licence attracts many applicants, and there is never any shortage of potential cooks. However, the Army is always short of clerks because few applicants feel it is worth wearing a uniform to push a pen.

Candidates have to provide their birth certificate, National Health number, National Insurance number, certificates of any educational or professional qualifications and a court memorandum or receipt of fines if applicable. They must also give the names and addresses of all relatives living outside England, Scotland or Wales. They also have to provide the names of 'two responsible people of good standing to testify that they are of good character'. (Women have to give three such references, but only two will be taken up.) These referees must be aged over 18, be in full-time employment, and able to report on the applicant in a professional capacity, e.g. a current or former employer, teacher, cadet unit commander or youth club leader. Referees cannot be friends, relatives or neighbours.

Female applicants undergo identical enlistment procedures to their male counterparts, but they cannot be employed in front-line combat roles. Within the military hierarchy there is a bizarre squeamishness about allowing women to serve in front-line regiments, a rather outdated view in my mind in a world where women have become multimillion pound airline pilots, managed international blue-chip companies and defied gravity to walk in space. Women continue to make some of the world's most formidable guerrilla fighters, helping to defeat the two great superpowers in Vietnam and Afghanistan. Women have become successful terrorist and suicide bombers, prepared to die for their 'cause'. Women who wish to serve in the Army need a well-developed sense of humour and the ability to give as good as they get.

The Army entrance tests have been updated somewhat in the last two years; the old pen and paper tests have been phased out for new touch-screen technology. The tests are split into five sections, with the applicant having to complete each section in a set time; the computer automatically moves on after the given time has elapsed. Each section consists of multi-choice questions, with the applicant pressing a coloured box to indicate the answer.

The five sections are: arithmetic, a basic numeracy test starting with addition, subtraction and multiplication, and moving on to more complex algebra, trigonometry and geometry; verbal, a test of vocabulary based on word association, in which a word is given and from the five selections the applicant has to choose the one that means the same; problems, a test of mechanical understanding and basic physics, each question being a practical problem; alphabet, a test based on the positions of letters of the alphabet; and finally literacy, a test of the applicant's understanding of spelling and grammar.

Many people, both in and outside the Army, question the validity of these tests at such an early stage, but the need for the selection staff to know the abilities of applicants at this point is certainly important in providing advice on possible jobs and trades. The majority of jobs in the Army require no academic qualifications, although for some technical trades, candidates need a minimum of four GCSEs at Grades A–C, including mathematics, English, a science and a practical subject like design technology. Moreover, having additional

8

qualifications does not exempt candidates from taking the educational tests.

Since the tests are multi-choice (three to five possible answers are given), all the candidates have an equal chance of success. Many consider the test too easy, while others think they are too hard; such comments show that the tests are not biased in any direction and they certainly do serve to match applicants to jobs more successfully.

When the tests are completed, the candidates are given a hearing test in a rather crude box in the corner of one corridor; inside is a chair and a pair of headphones. Each applicant sits looking through a window at a staff corporal, and raises the left or right arm to indicate in which ear the low-or high-pitched sounds can be heard.

After passing this test, the applicants receive the educational test results. The results are in the form of grades. The lower the score on the tests the better the grade; the top mark in each section is 1, which give a best possible total of 5. This 'total selection grading' is then converted into a 'sum selection grading'. There are a total of six sum gradings: SG-1, which represents the top 10 per cent of the population; SG-2, the next 20 per cent; SG-3+, which is an average and represents the next 20 per cent; SG-3–, which is below average and represents the next 20 per cent; SG-4, the next 20 per cent; and SG-5, which represents the lowest 10 per cent. Military statistics show that 60 per cent of the Army's manpower fall into the SG-2 and SG-3+ categories, and only 5 per cent are SG-1.

The selection staff give out the grades and passes. Any applicants who have failed to obtain the grade needed for their chosen trade or corps are advised on other options. The selection staff must be sure that each applicant will fit his or her chosen job and, before applicants can be enlisted, the staff need to know that they have the learning ability to pass the long and often difficult trade training. Candidates are given a computer print-out of all the eligible jobs available to them, and after three hours at the Careers Office they are given an appointment for their medical examination and sergeant's interview and leave with yet more pamphlets.

The Medical Examination

One of the most important aspects of a modern army is the
fitness of its soldiers; the need for them to be able to keep going
while on active service, or in extreme climatic conditions, for
days on end is paramount to successful operations. During
the selection process all potential recruits have a number
of medical examinations. The first is a brief check-over at
the Careers Office to ensure that there are no major health
problems. This is to ensure that at a later date the applicant
will be able to complete a set of basic fitness tests including a
$1\frac{1}{2}$ mile run. This is the basic standard for all troops, but it
is surprising how many serving combat soldiers fail this basic
fitness test or BFT.

The medical examination is a rather improvised affair
carried out by a civilian doctor. After they have stripped
to their underwear, the doctor checks the applicant's height
and weight, which should be in good proportion. (For a guide
to height–weight ratios see Appendix 2.) A urine sample is
taken and the doctor asks various personal questions. The
applicant's scalp, eyes, mouth, hands and feet are examined
for signs of infection, and the medical is completed with a
short strength test.

Many applicants fail this basic test, mainly because of
their standards of fitness rather than on medical grounds.
Army doctors and officers put this down to the lack of
physical education and sport in schools. As one captain
put it, 'Teachers are more intent on letting students get on
and play football than making them do circuit training or
cross-country running.' This may be true, but in a society
that puts more emphasis on educational qualifications than
sporting prowess, it is hardly surprising.

There are certain things that applicants could do to improve
their fitness before this and later examinations. Many are not
difficult: walking to and from work or school rather than
catching a bus; doing a short warm-up routine of stretches
each day; going for a short (1 mile) slow jog once or twice a
week, just faster than walking pace. Simple changes to routine
like this can improve general fitness by 30 per cent.

The most common problem Army doctors are faced with
today is asthma and in particular its onset during basic
training, when many recruits start running long distances for

the first time. There is no way in which an early examination can identify possible asthma sufferers, and the only ways military doctors can identify recruits with the problem are if the person suffers an attack during training or from medical records received from his or her civilian doctor. Owing to the confidential nature of these files, it is rare for them to be released from Army Manning and Records to local unit medical centres. Even if they were, they would only serve to confirm the illness after an attack. There are more in-depth medical examinations during a two-day visit to the Regional Section Centre at a local barracks and again at the start of basic training, but they are no better at spotting potential sufferers.

Opportunities for the Young

The Army has been accused of 'cradle snatching' by targeting the young for enlistment before school-leaving age. However, an adolescent faced with the prospect of unemployment or a training place on a very low wage is bound to find the salary of an Army Junior Leader, with the opportunity of learning a trade and gaining qualifications, an enticing choice.

Interested young applicants can visit the Careers Office from the age of 15, and they undergo the same selection process as adult recruits. Successful candidates receive an acceptance certificate, which guarantees a place in the Junior Army when they leave school. The Junior Army is very similar to the adult institution, with recruits spending two years at their chosen arm or service depot. Here they learn a trade and gain academic qualifications if they do not already have them, while trying for promotion within the junior rank structure. However, this structure seems to hold little weight in adult service, as is shown by the fact that only a few junior leaders who continue their service are promoted above corporal. A lance-corporal from the Queen's Royal Hussars, who reached Junior Regimental Sergeant-Major, said, 'After a while you get a bit sick of all the rank pulling . . . It's sad that the higher you go up the ladder the more crap you have to take when some Rupert cocks up.' He paused and smiled. 'At least at the bottom you can plead ignorance and get away with it.' He did, however, admit that the Army had changed his life and made him into a more confident and honest person. He explained, 'Coming from the Moss Side area of Manchester I was destined for a life of crime and prison. Joining the Army allowed me to get away from the deprivation and poverty, and gave me a chance to see countries people only dream about. I have gained trades and qualifications that were just not possible in Manchester. As a kid I needed an open door because I knew I could be something. The Army gave me that door and encouraged me to be what I wanted to be. If I had to go back and do it again, I wouldn't change a thing.'

The New Shop Window

As already mentioned the Front Line First review body suggested that recruit enlistment should be passed from Army Careers Information Offices to the Employment Services Agency and distributed between their 1,300 Job Centres. These would provide a filter before directing potential recruits to a new Defence Careers Information Office covering all three services. These would be regional offices manned by a small, centralised team of experienced staff. The Job Centre staff would explain to applicants the selection process and provide pamphlets and literature. The names and addresses of potential recruits would then be passed to the Regional Defence Careers Information Office.

There, the Army's selection staff would contact them and invite them to a non-obligatory talk with a staff member. If a firm application followed, applicants would spend a complete day at the Careers Office. What now takes five or six weeks would be completed during that day.

The educational tests and paperwork would be completed first and while the applicants were undergoing the medical examination the recruiting staff would be assessing test results and finding suitable jobs and trades. Applicants would then be called to one of the Recruit Selection Centres and the system would follow the same procedure as now. By cutting down the time recruits spend visiting and revisiting Careers Offices, it is envisaged that the cost per applicant would be reduced to £3,000.

This system would undoubtedly benefit the Army. Cutting down the applicant's waiting time reduces the possibility of recruits pulling out of the process after a night on the town with scornful friends. But although the idea of local Job

Centres being the first point of contact for applicants would appear to be obvious, some selection sergeants argue that it will do more harm than good. They claim that with the civilian population's bias against the military and lack of military experience, Job Centres may discourage potential recruits from joining. On the other hand, Job Centre staff are adamant that when the responsibility for recruitment is placed with them, their obligation is to provide the applicant with a wide choice of job opportunities, and to give fair, honest and unbiased advice and information. Some senior agency staff go one step further and pass the responsibility back to the Army; they point out that the only information they can provide the applicant with is that given to them by the MoD. But no matter what the argument, it is true that when the recommendations are implemented, some new training of staff will almost certainly have to be undertaken in Job Centres.

The fears of many recruiting staff are not uncommon, but the military have always viewed civilian involvement in military matters with suspicion and, more often than not, with resentment and hostility.

CHAPTER 2

The Selected Few

'The backbone of the Army is the
non-commissioned man!'
Rudyard Kipling, 1892

There is a growing need in the Army to cut down on recruit
wastage. A brigadier from the MoD said, 'The marked increase
in new recruits leaving the force inside their first 12 weeks is
worrying . . . We need to vet and interview recruits better
. . . to identify those who are less likely to stay the course.'
The knock-on effect of this view at local Army Recruiting
Offices is apparent. Gone are the days when 'gut feeling' was
sufficient to guarantee a recruit a place; now more emphasis
is put on interview techniques.

Today's recruiting staff are looking for applicants with a
good work record and a love of outdoor activities like camping,
canoeing and mountain climbing who enjoy learning and have
proved they can handle discipline. Today's recruits have been
school prefects, Army Cadet Force members or Territorial
Army soldiers. One recruiting sergeant remarked, 'Applicants
need to prove they can handle the stark realities of military
life and won't give up when the going gets tough . . . because
it certainly will do.'

The Sergeant's Interview

The sergeant's interview is conducted as an informal, fatherly
chat, which helps to relax the applicants and bring them out of
their shells. Interviewing sergeants are posted to the Careers
Office for two years. They are usually carefully chosen by their
regiments because they are bright and enthusiastic NCOs and
are likely to capture the imagination of the casual caller. The
sergeant skilfully prises answers from unsuspecting applicants
and within ten minutes will have weighed them up and know
whether they are likely to last the training.

'Interviewing is not a skill you learn or can be taught, it takes time and experience,' said one sergeant. 'You get a feeling about the person by the way they avoid your stare or fidget and twitch. Admittedly we all get nervous at interviews, some people can handle it and some can't; it's the ones who appear the most confident we look for.' This view is confirmed by other recruiting staff, who go further in asserting that if applicants are very nervous, they are less likely to settle into a disciplined life and will find it much harder to gain the confidence needed to survive.

The sergeant's interview is the last chance to ensure that all the paperwork has been completed and all the loose ends tied up. Personal information is confirmed and double checked, including possible debts – something that increasingly rules out many married men. There are acceptable limits; the rule of thumb is that the debt must be payable before the commencement of training, because most of the recruit's pay will be held back until he or she passes off; recruits receive only pocket-money to buy essential items. Normally anything under £500 is fine, but anything over this is considered unacceptable. Married applicants with mortgages are considered on their individual merits, but unless their partners are working there is little hope. If the partner is working, however, the question is often raised as to whether they are prepared to give up that employment to move overseas, to places like Northern Ireland or Cyprus, with no guarantee of work. If the partner *is* prepared to move, the applicant is back facing the question of financing the mortgage repayments during training; it is a vicious circle, with few options for breaking it.

Security and Other Checks

With the sergeant's interview over, the applicant is given an appointment date for the officer's interview. In the interim character references are taken up and security checks are made, which can take up to six months. Any possible offences are checked with the police Criminal Records Office.

In some cases credit reference agencies will be asked to investigate possible county court judgements, and positive vetting checks are conducted by Army Intelligence in cooperation with Military Intelligence Northern Ireland and the Royal Ulster Constabulary for any family links with paramilitary organisations. Relatives in the Republic of Ireland are also checked by the Irish police for the same reasons. If any connection with paramilitaries is found, whether the applicant knows about it or not, a refusal is guaranteed. Relatives in the armed forces are checked and a brief appraisal of their positive vetting papers may be requested for any omissions or discrepancies.

If the applicant originates from a Commonwealth country, these checks are carried out via the British High Commission in that country.

The Officer's Interview

While inquiries continue, the selection process proceeds and the officer's interview is considered the hardest part. A common comment from many applicants is, 'At the end of the day we are trying for a job and I'm asking him to put his faith in me and give me that job.'

The personnel selection officer who conducts the interview is usually a former warrant officer with more than 20 years' service, who has been promoted through the ranks and after receiving a late-entry commission has been promoted to Major. Mementos of his past experience fill the office in the form of regimental plaques, certificates and awards for merit. Silver figures of infantry soldiers take pride of place on the window sill, all inscribed with thanks for some service or deed.

The applicants are more often than not nervous and anxious, and the officer knows that trying to put them at ease is a futile task. He will speak in a slow, controlled and authoritative manner, like a solicitor counselling a client through a court-room battle. He will ask questions about candidates' past, present and future. He will find out their needs, what they are looking for from the Army and what they will give in return. He will probe their knowledge of their chosen regiment or corps, carefully guiding them to the correct answers with professional ease.

When asked what he is looking for, the Major pauses, deep in thought. 'I'm after a soldier, man or woman, who has some get up and go, is not scared to learn or change, enjoys sport and travelling; above all they need to be a team player, not selfish or arrogant.' He pauses and continues, 'The reality of modern warfare means killing, so the Army needs recruits who can learn self-discipline and obey orders.'

But what does the Army expect from recruits and what should they expect in return? 'We will give those who are chosen the opportunity to learn a trade and gain extra qualifications. They will travel the world on exercises and manoeuvres; we will give them the confidence and support to achieve anything. This year the Army has taken expeditions to Kenya, India, Australia and New Zealand to name but a few. They will also get good pay . . . maybe not the best in the world, but it is a lot more than they could hope for from a supermarket.' He picks up a copy of *The Times* and points to an article on British peace-keeping operations. 'Naturally there is a price to pay; we would expect them to go to any trouble spot in the world, to take part in humanitarian or peace-keeping operations, and they may have to defend British interests in some far-off country . . . They must realise that they will not only be subject to military law, but civilian law too; that they must be above reproach and honest.'

I asked if today's Army is better than before 'Options for Change'; the radical restructuring programme implemented to reverse the increasing resignation rate and the widespread equipment shortages, and if life had improved. 'The quality of life in the Armed Forces has always been what you make it, but admittedly there is a lot more to be done to improve certain aspects of life for single soldiers; these are currently being looked into and one can be sure they will be rectified in the future.' He added, 'Potential recruits who are currently entering the service are assured of an exciting and rewarding future, with a lot more opportunities for advancement and better recreational facilities.'

The officer ends the interview with a confirmation that the applicant will progress to the next stage of the selection process, which is a trip to the Army's Personnel Selection Centre. Applicants who get this far are still not guaranteed a place, but considering the same basic tests are completed at the Selection Centre under a military environment, it is safe to assume a final pass is likely.

Interviewing Tips

Anyone who wants to join the Army would do well to read about the history of their chosen regiment or corps. The more you know about its traditions, personalities and battle honours, the more convinced the interviewers will be that you are serious about joining.

Politeness is important. Although they do not necessarily expect it, it is advisable to address sergeants as such and officers as 'Sir'. You should be concise and never waffle, show that you have ambition and are keen to get on, but not too much. Saying that you want to be the next Montgomery will not impress your interviewers.

Be honest about your past, your family, your relationships and your future ambitions. If they feel that you are being honest they will give you a good recommendation. If they ask about weaknesses or failings, be frank and tell them; it shows that you have the ability to accept failure and the perseverance to try again.

Interviews always seem to end with, 'Have you got any questions you would like to ask me?' You should always say yes, and have at least one question ready; it shows that you are thinking and not just going through the motions. They do not have to be 'deep' questions. Something like, 'What are the opportunities for promotion within my regiment?' or 'Will I get the chance to complete further education courses while serving with the regiment?' will suffice.

Things you should not do include: chew gum; wear ear-rings; put your hands in pockets; appear despondent or uninterested (no matter how long you have to wait – the Army always keeps people waiting); and answer questions in monosyllables (yes, no, etc.). And *never* be late!

First impressions count, so you should wear smart but casual clothes. It must be stressed that this is only a general guide, however; you should wear what you consider appropriate.

Lichfield

New recruits are dispersed to their respective corps, or in some cases to a regional Recruit Selection Centre like the one in Lichfield; here the recruits are given a taste of military life over a 24-hour period. The Royal Electrical and Mechanical

Engineers, the Intelligence Corps and the Royal Corps of Signals prefer to do their own 'in house' selection, but wherever the recruit is sent the tests are similar.

Lichfield, with its two-platform railway station and historic cathedral, is a strange setting for a regional Selection Centre. The barracks are uninviting and the passing motorist rarely notices their existence, but for the would-be recruit, they are important. This is the only obstacle remaining before acceptance into the Army. Applicants start their visit with a lecture on behaviour at the barracks, then they complete a set of psychometric tests, not unlike those done at the recruiting office. Dinner is followed by a film about the life of a soldier and a trip to the Naafi bar, where age is irrelevant. 'If you're old enough to serve your country, you're old enough to drink' is a common comment made to the younger elements. Friendships quickly develop and alcohol is just as quickly devoured.

The accommodation is in four-bed rooms. Each bed-space has a plastic-covered mattress, two sheets, pillows and blankets, and a bedside locker covered in cigarette burns sits next to a creaking wardrobe on one wall.

Reveille is at six in the morning, with breakfast finishing at seven. Groans and muttered complaints of 'Middle of the bloody night' can be heard from beneath crumpled sheets. Before the day starts all bed linen has to be folded and arranged neatly. A brush, mop and cleaning kit are provided, but they are rarely used.

The Army has its own system for evaluating physical fitness, as it does for almost everything else. The infantry demand a grade A, which means a score of 110 in a series of physical tests. The main supporting corps require a grade B, the Medical and the Adjutant General's Corps require a grade C or D, while a grade E, which is a score of 50, is the basic standard every recruit needs to attain by the fifth week of basic training. To gain a pass from the Selection Centre, applicants must gain a grade P, which means they must complete three pull-ups to a bar, three dips on the parallel bars and seven sit-ups on an inclined bench. They must also complete a $1\frac{1}{2}$ mile run in under $10\frac{1}{2}$ minutes. Most of the recruits successfully pass the fitness test, albeit with some effort, but a few fail. NCOs shout encouragement while shaking their heads in disbelief, as the flagging recruits stumble forward holding their sides, their faces red and bathed in sweat as they falter on the edge of collapse.

After a shower and change of clothes the recruits are interviewed for the last time; most will be accepted into their nominated regiment or corps. Those few who fail the grade are given alternative regiments or advised on their failings and encouraged to try again; but few do.

The selected few receive confirmation of their acceptance within a week of returning home and are requested to attend an Oath of Allegiance ceremony. This is their last opportunity to back out. Once they have taken the Oath they are subject to military law, and failure to report for basic training could result in charges being brought, although this rarely happens.

The attestation ceremony is kept as informal as possible. When the applicants arrive, the attesting officer makes a point of calling them 'Mr' or 'Miss' on the way in and 'Private' on the way out. The young person stands facing the officer and with a small blue Bible in his right hand repeats the oath, phrase by phrase:

> I . . . swear by Almighty God that I will be faithful and bear true allegiance to Her Majesty Queen Elizabeth the Second, Her Heirs and Successors and that I will as in duty bound honestly and faithfully defend Her Majesty, Her Heirs and Successors in Person, Crown and Dignity against all enemies and will observe and obey all orders of Her Majesty, Her Heirs and Successors and of the Generals and Officers set over me.

The new recruit signs the B271B attestation form, is paid a nominal amount of one day's wages and reimbursed travelling expenses. From that moment he or she has become the newest member of Her Majesty's Armed Forces. The Major shakes hands and wishes him or her luck, knowing that becoming a trained soldier is not easy. Within two months the young recruits will have become members of one of the five Army Training Regiments.

CHAPTER 3

To be a Soldier

'Body and spirit I surrendered whole to harsh
Instructors – and received a soul.'
Rudyard Kipling, 1919

It is the last Friday in September. For many it is just another
ordinary day, but for 23 young men and women, it is a day
that will live in their memory forever. The drizzly rain has
been replaced by a harsh wind blowing from the open fields
on one side of the parade ground. Mothers and fathers,
brothers, sisters, girlfriends and boyfriends, all sit under
multicoloured umbrellas in their best suits and autumn
dresses. All around them officers and NCOs congregate
in small huddles, laughing and joking. The atmosphere is
punctuated by a shrill command followed by the distant
echo of marching feet; from a far corner the rank and file
of 7 Platoon, Army Training Regiment Winchester, stride
purposefully into view. The assembled gathering nudge, nod
and point out with pride their boys and girls. This Pass-Out
is the culmination of weeks of hard training. Along the way,
seven failed to make the grade and of these newest additions
to the British Army's Intelligence Corps, only four would
eventually go on to pass trade training first time and be
posted to units within the Corps.

The Pass-Out Parade is filled with protracted inspections
and predictable speeches, which few of the onlookers listen
to and even fewer care about. Later, there is a buffet and
drinks followed by photographs and chats with the smiling
platoon corporals. The former recruits are then off for
weekend leave. Many will relive their exciting memories,
while others quaff ten pints of beer with fathers and brothers
to show off their new-found skill of adulthood! However,
all this is a far cry from the timid and shy young boys and
girls that arrived at Winchester railway station some weeks
before.

Army Training Regiments

Recruits to the Army are sent to one of five Training Regiments to complete basic military training, depending on their chosen regiment or corps. They are:

ATR Glencorse, for the Scottish and King's Divisions.
ATR Lichfield, for the Prince of Wales's Division, the Parachute Regiment, the Royal Army Medical Corps, the Royal Army Veterinary Corps, the Royal Army Dental Corps and the Queen Alexandra's Royal Army Nursing Corps.
ATR Bassingbourn, for the Royal Engineers, the Royal Signals and the Queen's Division.
ATR Pirbright, for the Guards Division, the Household Cavalry, the Royal Artillery, the Royal Electrical and Mechanical Engineers and the Royal Logistics Corps.
ATR Winchester, for the Royal Armoured Corps, the Light Division, the Army Air Corps, the Adjutant General's Corps and the Intelligence Corps.

Basic Military Training

It is a hot, sunny afternoon in July as the Southampton-bound train pulls away from the platform, leaving behind ten fresh-faced new recruits. The stone-faced NCO strides purposefully forward, his civilian clothes unable to hide his profession. He mutters a few concise sentences in a harsh voice and the girls in the group are motioned away to a female NCO talking to a small group. She welcomes them with a forced smile and checks if they have brought sports bras and passport-sized photographs; those who have not are given 20 minutes to obtain them from a local shop and told that after that time transport will leave, with or without them. Meanwhile, the boys are ushered out to waiting minibuses.

The surrounding countryside is tranquil and peaceful, although few recruits notice the beauty when they first arrive. They are leaving behind the cosy civilian world and entering a strange and bewildering environment. Flowerdown Barracks is an up-to-date, modern military establishment, with newly built accommodation blocks that resemble any college or university. Each block is encircled with shrubs, herbaceous borders and lush, mown grass. The new arrivals enter the barracks and pass life-size infantry soldiers cast in iron, standing and kneeling in attacking positions. To the more observant, the spotlessly clean roads and paths are a sure sign of a highly disciplined institution.

With both male and female recruits completing the same initial training, 7 Platoon consists of twenty-seven recruits. Thirteen male and eleven female recruits are destined for the Intelligence Corps, and the remaining three are two potential officers for the Royal Green Jackets, who are completing an induction course before Sandhurst, and one Army Air Corps recruit.

It is surprising just how much care is taken over the way the recruits are received. There is a notable absence of intimidation by oppressive NCOs barking incoherent instructions; the days of such traditions have long since gone. The short, sharp, shock treatment was phased out after allegations of bullying and barbaric initiations, which undeniably occurred. Many an old soldier would argue that it was the only way to change boys into men, ready for the realities of warfare on the streets of Northern Ireland or the hills of Bosnia, but the Army now prefers a more relaxed approach.

All recruits joining the Army have to complete the Common Military Syllabus, whether their future is with the Royal Armoured Corps or the Royal Army Dental Corps; they are all infantry soldiers first and foremost.

The recruits are allocated bed-spaces. The men are accommodated in eight-man dormitories, separated by a tiled corridor leading to the washroom, toilet and shower facilities. The women are in a detached block, complete with secure key-code entrance locks to inhibit any would-be Romeos. Each bed-space comes with a single metal bed, a green-striped mattress, a fitted wardrobe and, if they are lucky, a bedside locker.

Those who have been expecting the worst are often surprised at the friendliness of all the permanent staff but for many others it is quite a culture shock: alone, isolated and with very few friends, the young recruits have to learn fast. Like a flock of sheep they follow each other around. On the first evening they sit in the lecture theatre in civilian clothes and are addressed by the Company Commander. He sets out the ground rules and explains what will happen over the following ten weeks. The Platoon Sergeant is introduced, along with the

23

NCO instructors, three men and one woman. They stand in their immaculate uniforms, complete with campaign medals from Northern Ireland, the Gulf and Bosnia. The attentive audience neither coughs nor fidgets as the officer reiterates that they will be trained to take their part in war and must be prepared to kill. For many, the thought of killing or being killed has never crossed their minds. The Major pauses for effect. It works; there is total silence.

The second and third days are filled with medical checks, documentation and a familiarisation tour of the barracks with the platoon corporals. Each recruit is issued with over £200 worth of Army clothing, and is told to mark each piece with name, rank and number.

It is late afternoon on the third day and many of the recruits are ironing their new green shirts and combat clothing for their first inspection, the smell of burnt starch ever present, while others polish and scrub boots and dirty lockers. Uniformity is slowly creeping in; all are wearing lightweight trousers, red PT vests and fashionable trainers, and all the males have Royal Marine style haircuts.

One of the platoon corporals moves from room to room, his Paratroop wings standing out, his red beret resting precariously above his eyebrow and hiding his tired and scornful look. He stops only momentarily to pass on instructions, 'Mummy's not here now, son, follow the trouser seam down . . . Johnson, what the hell do you look like? Put that beret in boiling water, leave it ten minutes then shape it. You look like bloody Gandhi!' The others laugh and share the joke, but the embarrassed recruit disappears to the washrooms to start again.

It is slowly becoming apparent that the NCOs possess Jekyll and Hyde personalities, and should be approached with care. The corporal picks up a pair of boots and explains, 'Remember lads, bullshit baffles brains. Now gather round and I'll show you the oldest tradition in the Army, apart from jumping your best mate's missus.' He pauses and laughter fills the silence. 'First we must get rid of the wrinkles, we can do this two ways . . .' The recruits watch in silent amazement as the NCO converts the boot into a mirrored replica of his own. They will spend endless hours buffing and 'bulling' their heavy combat boots, having to start again after each period on the drill-square. A wrong turn by another recruit can signal days of frantic 'bulling', as nowadays the unwritten rule that the culprit has to 'bull' the scarred boots is obsolete outside of Pirbright.

Friendships are beginning to develop and noticeable cliques are becoming apparent. The NCOs pair off the recruits to try to build up the 'buddy' system, constantly reiterating, 'To pass out you have to work together, you must be a team. No one can be a lone Jack in here and succeed.' The recruits are beginning to act and speak like squaddies. Expletives begin to enter their speech and they learn the jargon: they are called 'sprogs', food is 'scran', they eat in the 'cookhouse' and they sleep in 'pits'.

The first week is a gentle but exhausting start to their military lives. Their first room inspection passes with few words, but the instructors notice and mentally log every mistake. The first drill period is a clumsy affair. The platoon is arranged into a line from tallest to the shortest, and told to number off. Each number is cracked out like a rifle round: 'One, two, three, four . . . sixteen, seventeen . . .' Some recruits try to anticipate their number, only to stutter and fail; the punishment is ten press-ups and the process starts again. After many attempts the Platoon Sergeant barks, 'About bloody time, you sack of shit. Now listen. On my command, odd numbers one pace forward, even numbers one pace back.' He pauses to let it sink in and repeats the order, ending with, 'Go . . .'. The line breaks into a disorderly rabble as both odds and evens stand arguing over who is in the wrong.

The cantankerous Battalion Drill Sergeant watches from a distance, eyeing them with contempt. The recruits have stepped onto his sacred ground and perfection is all he is interested in. He stomps over to the pathetic platoon and, with all the old parade ground banter, dismisses them from the drill square. In time he will turn them from sloppy civvies to slick soldiers, but now is not the time.

The recruits are slowly learning the orderly life of being soldiers, with each of their locker layouts looking identical; toiletries carefully laid here, socks there and each shirt, pullover and combat jacket meticulously placed with each left sleeve draped over the next. Recruits have been taught how to make a bed correctly: sheets and blankets are tucked in with precise 12-inch nurses' corners, pillows fluffed up and counterpanes draped to hang 3 inches from the floor. For

many this discipline does not come easily, and the need for
the 'buddy' is now becoming apparent. One of the platoon
corporals is heard saying, 'There's no room for those of you
who prefer to do things on your jack . . .', but it is a point
that does not really hit home until the assault course and
log race.

There is no doubt that life has changed for the better
within basic training depots, and many of the improvements
are welcomed by the instructors, but one highly contentious
issue is discipline. Sergeants and warrant officers feel that
standards have dropped because of fears from the public
over bullying; many long-serving soldiers also feel that basic
training is not what it used to be and that in the long term
military efficiency will be affected. Nevertheless, few deny that
in the past there was a great deal of bullying and unnecessary
humiliation of recruits by their platoon corporals.

One reason for this bullying may have been that because
of manpower shortages, NCOs were promoted at a younger
age into platoon corporal positions which gave them direct
responsibility for younger, more vulnerable recruits. Because
of their own immaturity and insecurity, they felt they needed
to prove themselves and show their superiority. It is interesting
to note that there were few reported cases of bullying by
physical training instructors in training depots. These men
have successfully completed a gruelling physical course that
requires the ultimate in fitness, and they are respected for it,
so they have no need to prove themselves.

Senior NCOs did express concern about bullying at the
time, but they failed to get the support of senior officers until
it was too late and the Army was being dragged through the
tabloid press. One warrant officer said, 'When new guidelines
were issued and the training of recruits was improved, many
of these NCOs were returned to their regiments.' Since
'Options for Change' was implemented, most of them have
left the Army.

Instructors also confess that many recruits who should be
'back-squadded' or discharged from the Army are allowed to
continue on to their regiments. But with Army commanders
faced with rising resignations and falling enlistments, this is
unlikely to change. One instructor complained, 'The Army
has changed, in some areas for the better, but in others for
the worse. Some arrogant and obnoxious recruits need to be

taken behind the drill shed and slapped, but you just can't do that any more . . . Who's going to be there to pamper them on the streets of Northern Ireland, when some kid spits in their face or a sniper takes a pot-shot? Not me.' This attitude is not isolated; similar opinions can be heard throughout the Army, even more so in regiments which now spend more time having to 'mature' the new arrivals.

Officers are not surprised at this reaction, but they are somewhat indignant about it. One regimental adjutant said with some force, 'The Army is not saying that training depots cannot discipline recruits, but it has been stressed, in no uncertain terms, that bullying will not be tolerated . . . That does not mean they cannot take the recruit on a run, carrying 30-lbs of equipment in a backpack until he drops . . .'

Even without the intimidation, basic training is a serious jar to the system. With 6 a.m. starts and seventeen hours' training a day, all for no more than £1.50 an hour, the fantasy images of becoming overnight 'Rambos' are soon dispelled. Already 7 Platoon has lost two recruits; the rest struggle on with lectures on the structure of NATO, map-reading, field craft and small arms, while the ever-present NCOs conduct frequent room inspections.

The corporals call each room to attention as the Platoon Leader arrives. The officer is a new lieutenant with tours in Northern Ireland and Bosnia already under his belt. 'At ease, ladies,' he orders as he wanders from locker to locker, followed instinctively, like a child following its parent, by his golden retriever puppy. The officer stops and so does the puppy; the women's smiles are suppressed as the puppy sits obediently next to its master. 'What's that in your locker, Smith?' the officer says with disdain. The recruit turns her head slightly, and her expressionless face turns to a grimace. 'A pair of knickers, Sir,' she mutters, looking ahead and meeting the angry gaze of a female NCO. The displeased officer flicks the offending garment and it flies across the room, landing in a corner. The ever-vigilant puppy takes this as a cue to play and follows it through the air, pouncing and sliding as it hits the buffed tiles and the room fills with school-girl giggles. 'That will do,' the corporal barks and instantly the laughter stops. 'Smith, you will report to the Officers' Mess at seven every night for a week and take Harry for a walk.' The officer turns to the next locker. The puppy, by now bored, saunters off to find more mischief.

The Platoon Leader continues his inspection and moves to the next room, but the female NCO is not so tolerant; the recruits will face another room and locker inspection at 5 a.m. the next morning.

After the inspection the platoon is 'doubled' to the well-equipped gymnasium for a round of physical 'beasting' sessions. The physical training instructors no longer shout or scream at wavering recruits, but any faltering is punished by the whole platoon doing the exercise again or a set of press-ups. Unfit recruits are ordered on remedial PT. For one hour each night they have to do press-ups, sit-ups, shuttle runs and heaves to a bar; the PTIs guide and encourage while pushing each recruit to his or her limit and beyond. The Army's physical training programme no longer includes just circuit training and running; gymnastics, swimming, boxing, football, basketball and forced marches are the order of the day. Each Wednesday there is a sports afternoon, but cricket or rounders is out, replaced by 'murder ball' and 'killer frisbee'.

At the end of the ten weeks every recruit has to pass the combat fitness test. This consists of an 8-mile cross-country forced march, followed by a 200-metre dash carrying another recruit and ending with each recruit shooting accurately on the ranges. It is very rare that recruits fail this test; the high standards required by the PTIs during training ensure that they are fit to pass.

At the end of the third week the platoon is starting to improve in training; the embarrassing first visit to the drill-square is long since past and the Battalion Drill Instructor, with red sash and peaked cap, struts from one learning group to another. Even though he may be more muted than in the past, his presence is enough to cause sharper reactions in all recruits. The penalty for any mistake is a run around the drill-square, rifle aloft, shouting, 'I must not upset that nice drill instructor.' But with improvement comes the tightening of the screws and the NCOs increase the tempo.

The platoon has learned the basic soldiering skills of personal hygiene, washing, ironing, field craft, camouflage and how to assess firing distances. All recruits can read maps and use a prismatic compass. They have been shown how to stow equipment in their webbing and back-packs. They have learned basic first aid and the important nuclear, biological and chemical warfare skills. But now it is time for them to put all they have been taught into practice, during a two-day field exercise.

The Exercise

The 4-ton lorry drops the platoon 6 miles from the barracks in the local training area; the NCOs are on hand to issue orders and the squad moves off into a 2-mile forced march. The drizzly rain and blustery wind only add to the discomfort of the full webbing and 30-lb back-packs each recruit carries. The squad splits into four sections, with each section moving to a wet pine forest. Their training corporals begin instruction in living off the land, food preparation using 'compo' rations, building 'bivvies' to sleep in and digging shell scrapes – a task normally resulting in 3-ft-deep holes filled with peaty brown vile-smelling water, in which the recruits are forced to stand in for 2-hour 'stags' or sentry duties. The sections are taken out on patrols and practise their hand signals and movement across open ground. The sections have to remain operational and are told that a company of light infantry will attempt to ambush them – a lie that deliberately puts them on edge and guarantees many false alarms.

Many of the recruits will never have spent a night in the open before, most being city dwellers. The following morning, hungry and wet, the sections are gathered together and told that transport has broken down and they will have to march back to camp. The recruits' morale drops further. NCOs rally round and shout encouragement to those lagging behind: 'Come on Smith, you can do it', and 'Just another mile Smith, hang in there.' The march, although slow, is taking its toll on the recruits. Many are falling back with blisters and sprained ankles, and the platoon's Land-Rover is filling up fast.

One corporal sniffs at the recruits' feeble excuses for injuries and complains, 'When these lot finish training and move to their corps, the corps think we are to blame for the standard of soldier, but they fail to realise that there's only so much we can do. Beasting recruits is an answer, but it's the wrong answer. Training should be as realistic as possible; unfortunately realism is not yet important in today's training programmes.' He shrugs and stops to pick up another recruit.

The platoon is allowed the remainder of the day off; many sleep, others prepare their equipment for the drill test. The incentive for passing is a weekend's leave.

The following week is filled with drill and more drill. The morning rush for the hot shower and shaving mirror is followed by parade and block inspection; those who do not bother run the risk of being chastised by the ever watchful Platoon Sergeant. The drill-square is like no other part of the world; it fills all soldiers with a sense of dread. The memories of shouting out every movement by numbers – 'One . . . two, three . . . one!' – and the embarrassment of mistakes always send a shudder down the spine of even the most hardened of soldiers. The drill-square has an almost hypnotic effect; officers visibly grow 2 inches, warrant officers take on a new overbearing image and junior sergeants march with a swagger. The platoon is told that failure at the drill test will result in cancelled leave and extra drill over the weekend – a threat that is rarely carried out but is always a good motivator.

The recruit's day is filled with as many as seven lectures and just as many exercises; lunch is mainly spent preparing for the hectic afternoon schedule: gymnasium, firing range practice and more drill, each preceded by a frantic changing parade. The evening meal is gulped down and the recruits are back in their block, cleaning and shining for the company commander's inspection.

The recruits run from one room to another swapping and borrowing kit, and mops and electric bumpers swirl and buzz throughout the block. The air is filled with the smells of lavender air-fresheners and lemon toilet cream; gone are the old putrid odours of carbolic. The odd recruit manages a visit to the Naafi for a quick drink and phone-call home.

The next day, with the floors like glass and the beds unslept-in, the inspection goes well and the platoon is marched onto the drill-square for their first test. By mid-afternoon the railway station is filled with 7 Platoon waiting eagerly to go home, laughing and joking and happy that they are halfway through their training.

The 'Window' to Leave

Monday morning arrives with the return to the routine of inspections and lectures, but also, in the eighth week, the opening of the 'window'; a short period where recruits have the opportunity to leave the Army. Once the 'window' period is over recruits are committed to their term of engagement, usually three years. There are no takers from 7 Platoon. All the recruits are determined to succeed; the thought of going back to family and friends and saying they could not handle it keeps them going on.

The recruits are welcomed back with a weekend exercise, competing with 8 Platoon. The exercise is identical to the first, except that the recruits are on their own, and each section is commanded, not by a corporal, but by a recruit. Over the two days the role is rotated among the recruits to give the NCOs the opportunity to identify potential NCO material. The sections carry out infantry attacks on 8 Platoon and night navigation exercises.

The following week, fitness and drill are the priorities as the platoon corporals start preparing the recruits for the pass-off. Most military training units have an assault course, and all units consider theirs to be the hardest. What is not debated is that it is a test of strength and team-work. The muddy course is 800 metres long; between start and finish the recruits, working as a team, will have to navigate the 6- and 8-ft walls, the parallel bars, the 10-ft water-jump, the rope bridge, the scramble net and the zig-zag walls, all in a set time and while wearing full webbing and carrying a rifle. The PTIs' shouts of 'Go on, son, give it some stick!' and 'Are you going to let that bit of water beat you?' fill the air and have the effect of pushing on tired and bruised recruits.

Some of the obstacles might be considered easy, but the hot and exhausted recruits do not find them so. The pass rate is high, but there are casualties. The platoon loses two more recruits through injury, and by the end of the eighth week two more have gone: one potential officer is back-squadded because of a 'personality clash' with an NCO, and one recruit is dismissed as 'unsuitable for army service'. The platoon can only lose one more. Twenty recruits must pass off to meet the training regiment's returns; any less and questions are asked, a constant worry for the Platoon Commander.

In the platoon's last week the recruits complete tests in all the training subjects and take part in a three-day exercise, 'Final Fling'. They are also subjected to a gas chamber filled with CS gas. Dressed in full nuclear, biological and chemical warfare clothing, they have to walk around the chamber before removing their respirator and shouting their name, number, rank and date of birth. This is designed to force them to take a deep breath; they will not leave until they have. It always results in spluttering, coughing and spitting, with tear-filled eyes and burning throats, thus demonstrating how effective the respirator is!

The platoon will also have gone on an adventure training or outdoor leadership weekend. Here recruits go camping and take part in orienteering competitions, abseiling, mountain walking and canoeing.

After the Pass-Off

At the end of their basic training, the recruits, who ten weeks ago were considered the lowest of the low, have taken one step up the ladder. As newly trained soldiers they are now ready to start their Phase 2 trade training. For Royal Armoured Corps soldiers that will be as tank drivers; sappers go on to train as combat engineers; and infantry soldiers will enhance their fighting skills, skills that cannot be matched in any other regular army, and thus make the British soldier a formidable opponent to meet on the battlefield.

One recruit's opinion of basic training was: 'At first it wasn't as I expected, too easy really, boring too. I never expected to be bullied or anything like that – I don't think anyone does – but I did think it would be more disciplined.' Another said, 'The physical, and sometimes mental challenge was great, the NCOs were good, they knew what they were talking about and gave us a lot of confidence . . . The worst part was the inspections, it was like being treated like a bloody kid.'

The Platoon Sergeant is a 15-year veteran of military service in both the Falklands Campaign and the Gulf War, and is also Commando trained. His stony features hide a calm and unflappable character with an unimposing manner; he sums up his thoughts on basic training thus: 'The training we give recruits has been toned down. I don't feel that is a bad thing, but the onus for preparing these men and women for combat roles around the world is passed on to their regiments . . . Recruits leave here with a basic understanding of infantry skills, which is all they should leave here with. It is not the job of my NCOs to drum into new recruits how they should act as soldiers. When they go on the streets of Belfast or Sarajevo they will know their responsibilities to themselves and their comrades, but that can only come from their pride in their regiments and themselves. As a training regiment we can teach combat skills, but we cannot instil respect for the unit they fight with. Some units must be prepared to stop criticising training regiments and start doing their bit in the maturing of future combat soldiers.'

There can be no doubt that as the Army has changed, so has the training roles within it. No doubt it will take time for everyone to adjust to these new responsibilities, but adjust they will. Meanwhile the new soldier is off to trade training.

CHAPTER 4

Trade Training

'The courage of a soldier is heightened by his
knowledge of his profession.'

Vegetius, 378

The Army undoubtedly provides a diverse range of jobs
and trades for soldiers and many do not require formal
qualifications. In some regiments more than one trade
needs to be acquired to gain promotion; this extra skill is
a 'follow-on' trade. Some skills are similar to those needed
in civilian life, but others are unique to the Army. The
length of trade training varies according to the job the new
recruit has picked. Royal Armoured Corps soldiers undergo
an eight-week driving course at Wareham in Dorset before
posting to their regiments, while Intelligence Corps soldiers
complete a 26-week in-depth training programme at Ashford
in Kent.

The regiments and corps which make up the Army are
divided into two main groups: the Combat Arms, which are
responsible for the actual fighting, and the Services, which
provide the administrative and practical support. For some
soldiers, fighting will be their main job, so the trades and
qualifications they acquire will be in combat skills, while
others will be trained in a wide range of jobs leading to
professional qualifications.

Although women are not permitted to do front-line jobs
that involve combat, they are admitted to most regiments
in both the Combat Arms and the Services. The following
sections outline the jobs and trades that are available in all
the Army's corps and, in most cases, where this training is
conducted. For some specialist trades academic qualifications
are needed; normally these will be GCSEs in mathematics.
English and a science subject. Those jobs and trades that
are open to both men and women are marked with an
asterisk (*).

The Combat Arms

The Infantry

The Infantry (male only) is the largest of the Combat Arms and bears the brunt of most of Britain's combat commitments. The jobs available are: Infantry Soldier, Musician and Bandsman. Training is conducted at Winchester for the Light Infantry, at Pirbright, renowned for its drill parades, for guardsmen, and at Lichfield for parachutists. Other infantry soldiers are trained at Glencorse and Bassingbourn. Trade training for most infantry regiments is in advanced fighting skills and leadership. Infantry battalions may be armoured, air-Mobile or airborne and can be found in a wide theatre of operations. All infantry soldiers must be familiar with a vast range of weapons and battle strategies. Guardsmen posted to ceremonial duties in London or Edinburgh are also trained in infantry skills and to just as high a standard as the rest of the infantry, but they are also given the honour of being the Queen's ceremonial bodyguard.

The Household Cavalry

The Household Cavalry (male only) is part of the Household Division and famous for its ceremonial duties. But it also has a vital role on today's modern battlefield as a part of the Army's armoured 'heavy punch', and was the only cavalry regiment to fight in the Falklands Campaign. All soldiers are trained as both Tank Crewman and Mounted Dutyman, giving them a diversity of roles. The regiment on ceremonial duty first sends its soldiers on an equestrian course lasting 20 weeks. The first 16 are spent at Windsor and the last four in London, where they wear full dress uniform as much as possible and learn to cope with the busy traffic. The course includes lessons on how to walk the horse, how to trot, how to canter and how to jump 3-ft-high fences. It is very intensive, with the troopers having to look after their mounts as well as ride them.

The other side of the Household Cavalry, armoured reconnaissance regiment, sends its troopers on an eight-week tank drivers' and signals course. Then they are posted to a sabre squadron, and after 18 months they can complete their follow-on trade. If the regiment is in desperate need of any one skill, then both gunnery and driving trades can be completed immediately, and Household Cavalry soldiers have the advantage of obtaining a full driving licence but with the extra category 'H' qualification, which permits them to drive tracked vehicles, a very useful qualification if they leave the Army.

Advancement and promotion depends on completion of a Class 1 specialisation course in either driving or gunnery. Musicians are not trained in any combat skills, but are posted to a training depot for specialist musical training.

The Royal Armoured Corps
The Royal Armoured Corps (male only) provides the Army with both an advanced screening force and the powerful 'punch' needed on today's battlefield. Service is very similar to that in the Household Cavalry, although the soldiers do not carry out ceremonial duties. Soldiers are posted to their chosen regiment, which could be an armoured regiment equipped with Challenger tanks or an armoured reconnaissance regiment equipped with Scimitar CVR(T) light tanks. Trade training is conducted at Wareham in Dorset, with advanced Class 1 trades completed at Bovington. After joining their regiments soldiers can be posted to a sabre squadron or the Motor Transport Troop and obtain HGV and PSV licences. However, courses are in short supply and luck plays an important part in gaining a place. Bandsmen complete the same training as in the Household Cavalry.

The Royal Horse Artillery and The Royal Artillery
The Artillery (males and females) operates an impressive array of long-range weapons. Its vast range of job opportunities makes it one of the most sought-after regiments in the Army. Trades available are: Gunner Technical, as Surveyor*, Meteorologist*, Command Post Assistant*, Operator Artillery Intelligence* or Range Assistant*; Gunner Communications, working as either a Radar Operator or a Signaller; and Gunner Weapons, employed first as a Driver. Gunner Commandos are attached to 3 Commando Brigade (only the fittest will pass the Commando course), while Gunner Parachutists are attached to 24 Air-Mobile Brigade.

Mounted gunners for the King's Troop Royal Horse Artillery are considered to be the Artillery elite and recruits must be trained horsemen before joining. Trainees are sent

36

on a 6-month equitation course, where the standards of horsemanship are the highest in the Army. They must be able to gallop at 25 miles per hour on ceremonial rides while drawing a 1-ton gun and a ½-ton limber, both without brakes! All training is completed at the Royal Artillery Barracks at Woolwich and the duration of training depends on the trade taken, but is normally between ten and 22 weeks. Musicians are selected and trained as outlined above.

The Royal Engineers

The Royal Engineers (males and females) undertake a wide variety of construction projects and help the Army live, move and fight. It was one of the few corps to have some elements expanded rather than disbanded in the 'Options for Change' proposals. Jobs and trades available are: Engineer, Armoured Engineer, Amphibious Engineer, Bomb Disposal Engineer, Commando and Parachute Engineers and Combat Signaller.

For these trades, training is long and technical, but the Engineers have one of the lowest drop-out rates in the Combat Arms, which says a lot not only for the soldiers under training, but also for the experience and knowledge of the instructors and their ability to pass that information on without confusing the recruit.

Additional jobs available are: artisan tradesman, covering Bricklayer, Concreter, Carpenter and Joiner, Painter and Finisher, Plumber and Pipefitter, Blacksmith, Metalworker, Welder, Electrician and Construction Material Technician. Specialist trades available are: Surveyor, Draughtsman, Plant Operator Mechanic, Driver and Musician. Training for all trades is done at Chatham and lasts from ten to 20 weeks.

The Royal Signals

The Royal Signals (males and females) provide today's modern Army with the high-speed communications needed for the successful completion of world-wide operations. It is one of the most highly technical corps in the Army, with many specialist trades. Available trades are: Telecommunication Technician in Radio* and Systems*; Telecommunications Mechanic*; Telecommunications Operator in either Special*, Linguist*, Telegraph*, Systems*, Radio* and Radio Relay*; Driver Electrician; Driver Lineman; and Musician*. All training is carried out at the Royal School of Signals at Blandford and can last up to 32 weeks.

The Army Air Corps

The Army Air Corps (males and females) flies and operates all the Army's helicopters. Much of the trade training is carried with all the AAC soldiers* trained as groundcrewmen, which include flight servicing, flight tactics and basic flight training. This training also involves landing the helicopter in an emergency.

Ground crew can expect to spend at least two years with a squadron before they can apply to become pilots, and even then, only subject to the commanding officer's recommendation. They are then sent to the Aircrew Selection Centre at RAF Biggin Hill to assess their basic aptitude for the task. Those who pass are sent before the Pilot Selection Board. If successful they will proceed to pilot training, but the chances of promotion to helicopter navigator and pilot are slim; the road is long and the test extremely difficult. Only 5 per cent of AAC soldiers go on to become aircrew. Basic training is completed at Flowerdown Barracks in Winchester and ground crew training at Bovington in Dorset.

The Intelligence Corps

The Intelligence Corps (males and females) is the smallest of the Combat Arms and collects, interprets and circulates intelligence material to units for the successful completion of operations. Jobs available are: Operator Intelligence and Security* and Operator Special Intelligence (Analyst and Linguist)*. All operators follow the same initial training at Ashford in Kent, which takes just over four months and includes map-marking, clerical and communication skills, photographic interpretation, enemy vehicle recognition, basic signals and a language. Everyone must also pass the Army's Land-Rover driving skills course at Leconfield in Yorkshire. Linguists are then transferred to Loughborough to spend a minimum of one year learning a language; Russian, German and Arabic are the most common.

Trade training is among the hardest in the Army, but operators are promoted to Lance-Corporal upon posting to a field Army unit. The Intelligence Corps has the fastest promotion rate in the Army, and success depends on gaining additional qualifications. Soldiers from the Corps are sent on some of the best courses available in the Army to enhance their career opportunities and expertise, because 'intelligence is a growing business'.

The Services

The Royal Logistics Corps
The task of the Royal Logistics Corps (males and females) is to provide for the logistical needs of the Army. All basic training is completed at Pirbright and lasts ten weeks. Jobs available are: Air Dispatcher, Ammunition Technician*, Combat Driver*, Driver Radio Operator*, Catering Services Specialist*, Chef*, Movement Controller*, Musician*, Navigator/Seaman, Petroleum Operator*, Photographer*, Pioneer*, Port Operator*, Postal and Courier Operator*, Railwayman, Supply Controller*, Supply Specialist* and Vehicle Specialist*. All training is completed at the training depot in Deepcut, and it can be as short as eight weeks or as long as two years. Opportunities to gain City & Guilds certificates and NVQs are good and promotion can be fast, but normally not for three years.

Royal Electrical and Mechanical Engineers
The Royal Electrical and Mechanical Engineers (REME) (males and females) is the largest single 'cap badge' in the Army and maintains and services all the military hardware within the Army. Specialist jobs available are: Aircraft Technician*, Avionics Technician*, Telecommunications Technician*, Radar Technician*, Control Equipment Technician*, Instrument Technician* and Armourer*. Training is at the largest training establishment in the country, Arborfield near Reading, which also has the Apprentice College and the School of Electronic Engineering attached. Other trades available are: Gun-Fitter*, Metalsmith*, Shipwright (ship-builder)*, Vehicle Electrician*, Vehicle Mechanic*, Technical Storeman*, Recovery Mechanic* and Musician*. The duration of training depends on the trade, but it can be between ten and 32 weeks. There are good opportunities for NVQs, and City and Guilds certificates. Promotion can be fast, depending upon the trade.

Adjutant General's Corps
The Adjutant General's Corps (males and females) is a newly
created Corps resulting from the amalgamation of several
small corps and all the Army's clerks. One of the jobs available
is: Military Policeman/woman*. Basic and trade training for
the 'redcaps' is done at the training depot on the outskirts of
Chichester, in Sussex, and is split into three phases: Phase 1
involves military enhancement, signals, advanced map-reading
and outdoor leadership; Phase 2 covers police duties, military
law and the Police and Criminal Evidence Act; and in Phase
3 recruits put all they have learned into practice in mock-up
situations. They must also pass their Land-Rover driving
course. On completion of training, soldiers are promoted to
Class 3 lance-corporals and are normally posted to a garrison
in Germany.

Personnel and Financial Clerks* and Military Clerks*
receive their training, which lasts 12 weeks and includes
clerical and communications skills, filing and data protection,
at the main depot in Hampshire. Musicians* are trained with
the Household Cavalry.

Royal Army Dental Corps
The Royal Army Dental Corps (males and females) is one of
the smallest corps in the Army, and provides dental health
and hygiene for soldiers world-wide. The jobs available are:
Dental Support Specialist, Dental Hygienist* and Dental
Technician*. Two GCSEs at Grade C and above are required
for acceptance and training is conducted at NHS hospitals
before posting to a local dental centre in the UK or abroad.
Promotion is fast and there are good opportunities for further
academic advancement.

Royal Army Veterinary Corps
This is also a small corps, with both males and females
accepted. The trades available are: Animal Technical Assistant*, Dog Trainer*, Veterinary Technician*, Horse Master*
and Farrier*. Training is mostly at the Army's Equitation
Centre in Melton Mowbray, but the main training centre
for Army dog handlers is at the Defence Animal Support
Unit in Sennelager in Germany. Training lasts between 14
and 20 weeks. Promotion is considered slow compared to
other medical units, and it is also extremely rare for 'rankers'

40

to qualify as vets. There are good opportunities for further courses, but their allocation depends on the soldier's service time remaining.

Queen Alexandra's Royal Army Nursing Corps

Queen Alexandra's Royal Army Nursing Corps (males and females) provides a full professional nursing service and works closely with the Royal Army Medical Corps. Many recruits join the corps after completing a civilian qualification, but a few do so with no RGN status. Jobs available are: Student Nurse (General) RGN*; Registered Mental Nurse RMN*; Enrolled Nurse (General/Mental)*; Registered Midwife RM* and Health Care Assistant*. All training is undertaken in local NHS hospitals before posting to a military hospital for further training. Pay and promotion is linked closely to that in the NHS, with a few variations. Further qualifications are available, but course places are now few in number.

What Phase 2 Training is Like

After the hectic ten weeks of basic training, Phase 2 trade training is somewhat slower and more relaxed, but there is still a great deal of work to be done. Homework replaces the nightly rituals of cleaning parades and weekends are free, so many go home while a few stay and drink the weekend away at the Naafi or in local pubs and clubs.

The working day starts at 8 a.m. and finishes just after 4.30. Sports afternoons and the occasional run break up the monotony of lectures and practical tests. The mass of technical information that has to be absorbed is mind-boggling and not surprisingly a few decide that the Army is not for them and return to civilian life. The sergeant instructors are not bothered by this exodus, and shrug it off. One said, 'They join for an exciting life, not to sit in a classroom all day, facing death by vu-foil.'

The more determined stay and plod on. What makes many stay is the fact that they are within an institution of people that stand out from the rest. Those that return to their homes see their friends still on the dole or worse, heading for juvenile detention centres or prison.

For many recruits trade training is a time to swim in facts, figures and technical jargon; for others it is a hard slog from the start. However, upon completion and passing their individual trade, the door opens on a new world, the fascinating world of their chosen regiment or corps.

Follow-On Trades

All the trades and jobs we have detailed so far are the starting point for many careers. Each job, whether in the Infantry or the Intelligence Corps, gives the opportunity for further advancement or follow-on trades.

In some regiments, courses required for promotion are only offered after a set period of experience building has elapsed. In the Royal Armoured Corps this means that soldiers must complete 18 months of regimental service before being allowed to undertake a Class 2 trade, and a further 12 months before being considered for a Class 1 specialisation; and without both trades they cannot qualify for promotion. So in effect soldiers within some RAC regiments can expect to serve at least three years before being entitled to promotion.

This system was introduced in the late 1980s in response to increased disharmony in the lower ranks, as many senior troopers believed their juniors were being offered promotional courses, and in some cases actual promotion, before they had gained the necessary experience. However, the introduction of this rule makes a mockery of the Army's claims that soldiers are promoted on merit and their leadership qualities rather than on length of service. It is true that before the ruling was implemented some junior soldiers were promoted before their time, and that some did fail difficult follow-on trades because of a lack of experience, whereas an experienced trooper may have passed. But by introducing time constraints, the Army reduced the opportunities, and the incentives for the higher 'flyers', that 1 per cent of recruits who are a cut above the rest and would make superb NCOs and later competent senior WOs. It can only serve to demolish the enthusiasm of soldiers who are both professional and ambitious, and ultimately, I believe, increase the resignation rate of junior soldiers.

This rule is not applied in many other corps, in which the senior troopers do not have so much influence, most noticeably in the Royal Electrical and Mechanical Engineers and the Royal Signals, where soldiers are given almost total freedom to apply for any trade course that may enhance their expertise and promotional chances.

The Army has many extra courses available, although many of the specialist ones are restricted to sergeants and above. Within each regimental headquarters there is an annual course folder and all soldiers are allowed to look through it and apply for those courses that are open to them. Courses include adventure training in hill walking, skiing and novice to advanced rock climbing. There are also the more military-based courses, including the Long-Range Patrol Course (normally only open to infantry and reconnaissance troops) and the harder and more specialist Resistance to Interrogation Courses held at the Joint Services Interrogation Wing at Ashford. The Army runs over 170 courses a year in addition to the normal regimental trade training, so there is normally one to suit every soldier, and they are free.

Further Education

There are education centres in most barracks in the UK and Germany. Run by officers from the Adjutant General's Corps, they provide soldiers with the opportunity to retake GCSEs and A Levels. They are well equipped and provide excellent facilities for the students. Most also have in-house libraries. The officers who run and teach the courses are not the usual rank-conscious subalterns but experienced and qualified teachers; many have long experience in secondary education before serving with the Army. The education centres also have other courses that could be of interest to soldiers, from the Educational Promotion Certificate (needed by all would-be sergeants) to advanced German or Arabic, business degrees and NVQs in management. The Army Education Centre also prepares soldiers who are leaving the Army with administration and resettlement courses.

Support Services soldiers are the most likely to take advantage of the education centres. This is not due to any lack of interest from Combat Arm soldiers, but because Support Services soldiers are less likely to be deployed on exercises or six-month tours of duties in Northern Ireland. However, the Combat Arm soldier's difficulties can be overcome with the help and advice of the centre staff, normally by setting the course in modules. The student just needs to complete each module before moving on to the next. Most of the courses can be done this way, with the student doing the work in his or her own time. If advice or explanation is needed, a phone call or visit to another local education centre can solve the problem. In operational areas like Bosnia, where there are no such facilities, the student can put the course on hold and resume it upon returning. It is a good scheme and has had many successes.

Despite this, few combat soldiers take the opportunity to advance their academic qualifications, and there is another reason why they will not take the plunge other than simply a lack of time. More often than not it is the fear of being called a 'cissy' for going back to school. In a macho environment like the military, doing GCSEs goes against the barrack-room culture and exposes the soldier to ridicule by those who would prefer to criticise and do nothing rather than praise and do something.

The Army can provide a wide selection of courses. Some can help promotion, others self-development or personal reward. As one officer said, 'The Army is an adventure; courses are just an added bonus.'

CHAPTER 5

Officer Entrance

'The badge of rank an officer wears on his coat
is really a symbol of Servitude – Servitude to
his men.'
General Maxwell D Taylor, 1953

Imagine for a moment you are lying down looking up at the deep blue tranquil sky. The hot baked sand beneath you fills your body with warmth and the air is still and quiet, but within seconds your peaceful world erupts into mayhem and confusion as your head is filled with the sound of anti-tank rockets being fired from nearby, and in the distance the 'carump' and dull thud of explosions hitting their targets. 'What are your orders, Sir?' you hear your Platoon Sergeant shout, but the words are alien to you, he cannot be talking to *you*, can he? You bring your eyes back to earth and you are immediately filled with terror and fear. Your platoon of 30 highly trained and experienced soldiers awaits your orders, but this is no training exercise on Salisbury Plain or the Hohne Ranges. This is real, this is Iraq, this is *war*.

'What are your orders, Sir?' The sergeant's voice now sounds more determined and angry. You try to think, but fear swells deep inside your stomach. You stare at him and see his rising anger; his head darts from left to right as he checks the platoon, *your platoon*. You try desperately to think of your Sandhurst training, and all that they drummed into you day after day, but your mind is blank. You snap your eyes shut, trying to block out the terror, but your head is filled with one word; over and over again, it thumps about your head, *leadership, leadership*!

You snap upright and grasp your sergeant's arm. His eyes snap to meet yours. 'Yes, Sir?' You are now thinking more clearly, your thoughts back at Sandhurst. The words of the senior instructor ring in your head. 'You are the leader of your men, *you* and you alone, and you must suppress your own fear and give the orders.' You look deep into the platoon sergeant's eyes, knowing you are sending many men into battle, the men *you* trained, *you* prepared for war. 'Sergeant, the orders are . . .'

The ability to give the orders that may send good soldiers to their deaths is what separates the officers from the soldiers. Many NCOs feel that giving such orders is easy, but in the heat of battle, few would be prepared to give them, let alone lead their men from the front. It takes a special kind of courage to suppress fear and lead by example in war, but all officers must be prepared to issue orders and lead their men into battle, and accept the responsibility if it fails. Could you?

The Army needs men and women who can accept responsibility at an early age. Officers have to lead 30 experienced soldiers daily; the need for high standards of physical fitness and intellect goes without saying, but potential officers also need to understand that they will be despised and envied by many of the soldiers they command. This is not due to any personal animosity, but to the fact that many soldiers feel that officers have an easy and pampered life.

Many serving officers fail to understand that they have to earn the respect of the soldiers in their platoons. Officers who feel they have earned the right to respect after completing their Sandhurst training are gravely mistaken, and are soon brought down to earth on arrival at their regiment. It cannot be denied that simply receiving the Queen's commission entitles officers to some respect, but earning the full respect of the men and women in their platoon takes time and a great deal of hard work.

For this simple reason officer selection has to be thorough, with experienced staff officers paying meticulous attention to every detail, including attitude, confidence and aggression, during the three-day tests completed at the Regular Commissions Board.

Entry Requirements

There is no particular 'officer type', mainly because of the variety of roles and appointments that are available to all potential officers, but the Army does look for those who can stand up for what they believe in, can express themselves easily and clearly, demonstrate that they have a mind of their own and are not easily led, because being an officer brings with it a great deal of responsibility.

The percentage of potential officers coming from public-school backgrounds has dropped considerably in the last ten years. The old ethos of an officer elite drawn from the 'old school tie' set has all but disappeared. The number of entrants from public schools, after falling to a record low, has steadily increased, and is now on a par with those from state schools.

The Foot Guards and Household Cavalry regiments only accept a certain type of officer – often, but not always, rich. However, they say this is due to the enormous cost of regimental dress uniforms and ceremonial paraphernalia, particularly when posted to guard duties at Buckingham Palace. With the shabrack, the richly embroidered saddlecloth, costing in excess of £2,000 and with cavalry officers paying over £1,000 for a charger, few can afford the costs. It is also common for Household Cavalry officers to donate an item of value to the Officers' Mess; solid silver statues or commissioned paintings of historic regimental battles are the norm. Officers also have such extra-mural activities as polo, show-jumping, hunting and shooting, so being a member of this elite is an expensive business. Officers in other regiments and corps, however, do not have this kind of expense.

Candidates wishing to apply for a career as a commissioned officer will rarely start by visiting the local Army Career Information Offices or Job Centres, but will contact friends or relatives who have served within the armed forces. After gaining a general idea of what is involved, most young hopefuls cut out and send off the coupons from colour supplements.

These coupons are processed by a civilian handling company in Bristol, which replies with a personalised letter and encloses a comprehensive information pack and application form. Applications are normally followed up by the Schools Liaison Officer, usually a senior retired officer; candidates can also contact him direct via the school careers staff.

Potential officers must first decide which regiment or corps they wish to join. The regiment is then approached to sponsor the candidate through the officer selection process, which is normally a formality. Regiments process the application and arrange Pre-Regular Commissions Board briefings. This does not mean that they are offering a vacancy; owing to the uncertainty of the Regular Commissions Board (RCB) hurdle, many regiments sponsor more applicants than they have vacancies for, and some regiments that have no shortage of applicants, like the Parachute Regiment, can actually refuse Short Service Limited Commissions and some Short Service Commissions unless the candidate is considered exceptional.

Potential officers who are undecided about their choice of regiment and have acquired more than one sponsorship do not have to make their final decision until they have completed the Royal Military Academy Sandhurst course. Regiments often invite potential officers for informal visits, in the hope of confirming an application before Sandhurst, when they are more susceptible to change. On their visits they are shown the plush Officers' Mess where they will live, introduced to important regimental figures and taken out on an exercise for a couple of days. This allows both parties to assess each other for suitability.

The Army has six methods of entry for both male and female potential officers, including three types of Queen's commission, but everyone must complete the selection process, including the Pre-Regular Commissions Board, the RCB and training at Sandhurst. Female officers are now permitted to serve with most Army units, but attachment to front-line combat regiments like the Household Cavalry, the Royal Armoured Corps and the Infantry can only be as Assistant Adjutants for a two-year posting. All officers obtain their commission upon completion of the Royal Military Academy Sandhurst course.

Types of Commission

Regular Commission (REG C)

All applicants attend the commissioning course at Sandhurst. Entries to Sandhurst are in January, May and September, and applicants hold the rank of Officer Cadet whilst training. This is then followed by the young officer's course appropriate to their arm or corps. On successful completion of the course, candidates will receive the pay of their rank back-dated to the date of their entry to Sandhurst. All officers must complete a minimum of three years' commissioned service (six years for the Army Air Corps). Age limits for entry are between 17 years 9 months and 25 years on entry to Sandhurst. Some

48

candidates who hold a degree in a relevant profession may be considered up to 27. Candidates should have a minimum of five A–C passes at GCSE or equivalent in approved subjects, which must include mathematics, English language, and either a science subject or a foreign language. In addition, they need at least two passes at A Level at Grades A–E or equivalent. Some specialist jobs in the Royal Electrical Mechanical Engineers and the Training Services Branch of the Adjutant General's Corps are only open to graduates with the appropriate degree or professional qualifications.

Short Service Commission (SSC)

This is identical to the Regular Commission except that A Level passes are not required. Only Grade A–C passes at GCSE equivalent in five separate approved subjects which must include mathematics and English language are needed. Some regiments and corps require candidates, particularly non-graduates, to meet higher educational qualifications. Terms of service are for a minimum of three years' commissioned service (six years for the Army Air Corps), extendable, if mutually agreed, to a maximum of eight years. After two years an SSC officer may apply to convert to a Regular Commission.

Short Service Limited Commission (SSLC)

This is a 'gap year' commission open to school leavers who have time to spare before taking up a firm place at a university or college of higher education to read for a recognised first degree. They must first pass the RCB. Successful candidates complete a three-week introductory course at Sandhurst and serve for a minimum of four weeks and a maximum of 18 months. Courses start in October, November, January and February. Candidates must be 18 but under 20 on the day of commissioning, and must give six weeks' notice to terminate their commission. There is no reserve liability and no subsequent obligation to serve in the Army.

Scholarships and Sponsorships

The Army Scholarship Scheme

This scheme is open to applicants between the ages of 16 and $16\frac{1}{2}$ and allows those chosen to study for their A Levels.

There are two competitions for entry each year, in spring and autumn. The competition is stiff, with only 90 places awarded each year, and most scholars go on to apply for an undergraduate award, either a cadetship or a bursary, and read for a degree before attending the Sandhurst course.

Shortlisted candidates will attend a preliminary board at Sandhurst in March or October, which will select those to go forward to the final assessment held at the RCB at Westbury in May and November. Candidates must normally be sitting no less than seven subjects at GCSE or equivalent and must be confident of passes at Grade A–C in English language, mathematics and a science subject or a foreign language. Of all the subjects taken, four must be of Grade B or above. Candidates need to achieve at least 14 points from their grades, where A=3, B=2 and C=1. Applicants must also have at least one full academic year left before applying and have the potential to gain a minimum of two passes at A Level or three at SCE higher grades.

Army scholars are not required to attend the RCB. The scholarship carries with it a financial award, paid each term until the Upper Sixth year, with a commitment by the recipient to serve for a minimum of three years as a REG C officer after commissioning.

Welbeck College
Welbeck College provides a two-year science-based A Level syllabus for both boys and girls interested in joining one of the Army's Engineering or Technical Corps. A place at Welbeck guarantees entry to Sandhurst and many go on to study for degrees at the Royal Military College of Science, Shrivenham or to read engineering at Oxford or Cambridge where tuition is free. Candidates must normally be aged between 15 years 9 months and 17 years 6 months on the day of entry into the college, and must have achieved, or be expected to achieve, Grade C or better at GCSE or equivalent in mathematics (the higher level syllabus, in Scotland credit level), physics (or a subject including physics), English language and two further subjects before their date of entry to the college. They must be considered capable of successfully undertaking the A Level course in three subjects, which must include mathematics and, preferably, physics. Shortlisted candidates appear before a Selection Board held in February for the September entry,

or July for the smaller January entry. Girls can only join in September. Successful completion of the Welbeck course exempts candidates from attendance at the RCB.

Undergraduate Cadetships
Cadetship holders at universities or colleges are commissioned as Army officers on probation and paid at a special rate. In return they are committed to serving as regular officers for five years after completing Sandhurst training, and whilst studying they must be active members of the university Officer Training Corps and carry out attachments with their sponsoring regiments or corps in the long summer vacation. Candidates must be aged over $17\frac{1}{2}$ on 1 September of the year of entry and must graduate and enter Sandhurst before their twenty-fifth birthday. Candidates must have a confirmed place to read for a recognised honours degree at a university or college of further education or be reading for such a degree but not have started the final year of the course. Cadetships are not awarded to applicants wishing to study overseas.

Cadetships are awarded in late August with undergraduate cadets attending a ten-day pre-university course at Sandhurst at the beginning of September in the year of the award. Competition is strong and academic standards high. Priority is given to those reading engineering- and technology-related degrees.

Bursaries
Bursaries are identical to undergraduate cadetships except that bursars are not commissioned whilst studying. Instead they promise to serve for three years once they have completed the course at Sandhurst. In return the Army pays them a financial award to supplement their grant whilst they study. For bursaries any subject is acceptable. Bursaries are awarded in September and October, with some available in January and April.

Professional Qualifications and Special Cadetships
Some specialist corps provide limited opportunities for those who wish to join from the professions, or wish to study for professional qualifications.

The Royal Army Medical Corps awards medical cadetships to selected candidates who have passed their second MB or equivalent exam, who have started clinical studies, or who are within three years of qualification below the age of 25. The Royal Army Dental Corps awards dental cadetships to dental students who are within the final two years of study. Entry is also open to all qualified dental practitioners. The Army Legal Services Branch of the Adjutant General's Corps has limited openings for its legal cadetship scheme. Commissions in the rank of Captain may be awarded to qualified solicitors or barristers between the ages of 24 and 30. Queen Alexandra's Royal Army Nursing Corps has openings for qualified RGNs with at least one year's post-registration experience. Candidates are commissioned as nursing officers. And the Royal Army Chaplain's Department takes graduate clergy who should normally have served at least one curacy and be under 34.

The Pre-Regular Commissions Board Briefing

All potential officers, regardless of type of commission, have to undertake the Army's selection procedure, including the Regular Commissions Board. With just over 1,000 candidates per year and approximately 650 Short Service and Regular Commissions available, the RCB is a tough mountain to overcome.

Regiments or corps first invite their candidates to attend a Pre-Regular Commissions Board briefing, which lasts two or three days and is designed to familiarise applicants with the wide-ranging selection tests and interviews that the RCB conducts. This briefing is not the first stage of the selection process, but an aid to help the candidates pass the RCB, and none of the results of this briefing are passed to the Board. It is the Regular Commissions Board alone that will determine whether the applicants are acceptable for an Army commission and ultimately military service.

The briefing is broken down into mock interviews and written tests, and candidates are given orders to interpret and carry out within set groups. It is conducted in a relaxed and informal environment, with staff officers advising and explaining all the time. There are none of the frantic shouts and endless scribbling that are the hallmark of the main Board. For many of the applicants, this is the only opportunity they will get to refine their leadership potential and confidence; once they start the RCB test days, the time for such fine tuning will be over.

The Regular Commissions Board (RCB)

All candidates for a commission in the Army, with the exception of those holding Army scholarships or professional qualifications and Welbeck College graduates, have to complete three and a half days of exhaustive tests set by the RCB at Westbury in Wiltshire.

Leighton House, with its muddy obstacle course and brightly painted scaffolding, is surrounded by seasoned parkland filled with trees and lush green grass. The trees cast seas of shadow across the Victorian conservatory and Officers' Mess and give it a still and peaceful atmosphere. The newly arriving candidates might be forgiven for thinking that their stay will be easy.

The newly painted accommodation blocks flank one side of the gravelled road leading to the main building and are laid out in neat rows of graceful symmetry. The only other visible clues to any military presence are the signs, painted in traditional army red, showing directions to important areas. A few have strange and confusing symbols, the first indication that all is not as it seems!

Forty-eight candidates are tested at a time, divided into groups of eight. Each group is identified by a colour and each applicant is known only by the number worn on his or her chest, like a speedway rider.

A brigadier serves as President of the RCB; under him are three colonels, each responsible for examining two groups, and each group has a leader who is a serving major. Candidates are treated as officer cadets and have their own mess hall and drawing room for relaxation.

Each candidate is carefully assessed on training potential, practical ability and character. The procedure is a tried and tested one, dating back to the Second World War, which has been improved over the years by Army psychiatrists. The candidates complete a set of intelligence tests, a written test on general knowledge and a set of essays on given subjects. Meticulous marking, and the applicant's anonymity, rule out the possibility of personal feelings affecting the grades given.

The tests many candidates fear most are the individual command tasks. For example, a weighted oil drum may have to be moved across an improvised ravine using ropes, planks and barrels. The applicant has to plan, instruct and control the crossing in a given time, while being observed by an ever-watchful officer who rarely speaks; his eyes scan the applicant and observe the others for signs of frustration, annoyance and panic. The applicant tries desperately to succeed, while hiding the fear of failure.

The 'flappers' and those who are officious are soon spotted and are doomed to failure, while the calm and spirited complete the task and move on. A catastrophe like the party falling into the canyon or the oil drum being left behind do not amount to instant failure, but they make the officer watch more intently for the reactions of the group and the leader. Will the leader panic, blame others or give up? The officer adds to the pressure by indicating when one minute remains and a burst of activity erupts. Some members of the group turn into 'headless chickens' while others shrug and laugh it off. Whether the group has succeeded or not is not the issue, but during this short space of time each one will have shown a small piece of his or her potential leadership and over the remaining command tests the officer will build up a faultless picture of the potential commanders and the confident bluffers.

The Board is not looking for brilliant individuals but for those who are generally good all-rounders, and who have intellect, common sense and personality. The tests help identify those who can think clearly and confidently when under pressure.

The potential officer's personality and common sense are assessed both on the command tasks and during group discussions on current affairs; Northern Ireland, Bosnia, economics and the environment are the current favourite subjects. People's political viewpoint is not important, but clear debate is. The supervising staff watch with interest for those who refuse to listen to others, those who irritate and the few who switch off and say nothing. Potential officers who side-step difficult issues by saying 'I don't understand the subject sufficiently to discuss it' are frowned on by the selection officers. The applicants also have to complete the standard military assault course during their stay.

On the final day all applicants have a set of formal and informal interviews, preceded by a five-minute lecture on a given topic. Each candidate is called in turn and given a subject to lecture about. It could be anything from the candidate's past, taken from the CV which he or she submitted earlier. This is when candidates really have to think on their feet, and the lecture styles vary from the comic to the modest and bashful.

After the applicants have left they are assessed on 17 different qualities, with five grades for each quality: strong, good, adequate, limited and weak. One 'weak' could be enough to fail an applicant, as could five or more 'limiteds'.

The Board base their assessment on the evidence from three sources. The first is performance at the RCB, the second is experience of life so far and includes academic qualifications, and the third is the intelligence tests completed soon after arrival at the RCB. On the basis of these tests the applicant is given an Officer's Intelligence Rating (OIR), on a scale of 0–10, for the purpose of assessment at the end of the three days. An OIR of 10 or 9 is classed as 'strong', an OIR of 8 as 'good', an OIR of 7 as 'adequate' and equal to an IQ rating of 120–125 on the national scale, an OIR of 6 as 'limited' and an OIR of 5 or below as weak. The OIR scores are the most important single source of evidence; applicants who lose their head or explode with rage are usually found to have a low OIR.

It is rare for an OIR of 5 to be accepted, and someone with an OIR of 4 or below, the standard of an average lance-corporal, is never accepted. At the other end of the scale, an OIR of 10 is only awarded once every two years, although there may be at least one candidate able to achieve the grade on each intake.

Applicants are notified of the RCB's verdict by letter within three days of their return home. They could either have passed, failed, or failed with the recommendation they try again. All applicants who complete the RCB are given a final grading. For those who pass, this is kept confidential and will form the basis of the potential officer's career. All confidential reports must match or better this score. An A means the candidate will make an outstanding officer, and perhaps understandably this grade is hardly ever given. A B indicates that he or she should make a very good officer, and a C indicates good officer material. The most common grade is D which indicates to Sandhurst that the applicant is adequate. The last grade is E, which signifies that the applicant has been given the benefit of the doubt, but is considered a risk. There are three types of E grade, each denoting an area of risk: immature, education and character.

Those applicants who fail are graded F, and the few who have proved so disastrous that the RCB never wants to see them again are graded FF. This grade, however, can only be awarded by the RCB President.

Those that pass the RCB are recommended for a place at the Royal Military Academy Sandhurst, but those who are considered borderline cases are sent on a 12-week course to Rowallan Company at Sandhurst. Here the candidates concentrate on adventure training activities like rock climbing, canoeing and hill walking, all designed to build character. A few are sent on an O-type commission course as potential officers with new recruits starting basic training at various depots around the country. This course is usually undertaken by candidates who are unsure of their final unit, or on the instructions of their regiments, so that they can assess them.

There are some candidates who use the offer of a Queen's commission from the RCB to give them greater credibility in the civilian world, especially when negotiating with top companies for employment. Each year just over 10 per cent of applicants offered commissions in the regular Army fail to arrive at Sandhurst for training. With the cost of attendance at the RCB running at well over £1,000 per applicant, this is not only a waste of good potential officers, but more importantly, a waste of money needed elsewhere in the Army. The directing staff admit, however, that there is no way to eliminate the problem, and the Army has come to accept it as one of the legacies of modern society.

Modern combat training ensures soldiers can adapt and overcome any obstacle. Here soldiers attempt a river crossing during exercises in Germany. *(Soldier Magazine)*

The British Army can expect to be deployed on more peace-keeping operations under the United Nation's banner. Like this Warrior crew in Bosnia shortly before coming under NATO control. *(Soldier Magazine)*

Ceremonial duties are an integral part of a soldier's life. Here a trooper from the Queen's Life Guards sits on parade outside Horse Guards Parade.

The Challenger tank provides the army with a powerful punch, as proven during the Gulf War. Such power is only achievable with the professionalism of its turret crews, seen here during exercises on Salisbury Plain. *(Soldier Magazine)*

Warriors prepare for war. A troop of armoured fighting vehicles from The Prince of Wales' Own Regiment of Yorkshire practise their advance-to-contact drills prior to deployment. *(Soldier Magazine)*

KAPE teams, like these Scimitar crews (*above and below*), are often the first direct contact many potential recruits have with the army.

Bosnia, the reality. Soldiers feel it is closer to Vietnam in the 1960s than Europe in the 1990s and regiments can spend in excess of six months here.

Soldiers must be prepared to work in any climate in any part of the world, including the hot deserts of the Gulf or the freezing temperatures in Norway.

Stuck again! Even a modern army cannot control the elements and soldiers must always be mobile. (*below*) Back on the road again and ready for another day of peace-keeping.

As the sun sets over the Canadian prairies, the Queen's Royal Hussars cavalry regiment prepares for live firing exercise. The Challenger tank's advanced night-fighting capability now makes warfare a 24-hour reality.

A Challenger fires smoke to cover its withdrawal during a 'hot contact' on Salisbury Plain.

The Passing Off parade is the culmination of weeks of intense training in the basics of military life and survival, but now it is time for the real work to begin.

Time to show off in front of relatives, and feel proud *To Be A Soldier*. NCOs of the Queen's Royal Hussars parade for a comrade's wedding.

CHAPTER 6

Sandhurst

'This Academy trains future regular officers
to command and lead the finest soldiers in
the world.'
Major-General F R G Matthews, 1947

Screams at 6 a.m. Terror. Relief. Anger. Reprimands. Guilt.
Just the start of another day for the officer cadets at
the Royal Military Academy Sandhurst. Their 11-month
commissioning course is the equivalent of the recruits' basic
training, but here, in the Edwardian surroundings of New and
Old College the cadets will endure hardship, humiliation, pain
and self-sacrifice, all for the glory of being an officer.

Sandhurst, near Camberley in Berkshire, is surrounded by
over 900 acres of beautiful rolling countryside, and filled
with lush green meadows, lakes and woods. The Academy's
mystique is only heightened by the imposing Grand Entrance
of Old Building, which contrasts to the modern ugliness of
Victory College. The old temporary buildings have been
replaced by purpose-built blocks that now house over 1,600
cadet officers.

Apart from the three intakes a year on the standard
commissioning course for cadet officers, Sandhurst is responsible for many other courses, including the Territorial Army
and Army Cadet Force officer training courses; the profes-
sionally qualified officers' course for doctors, lawyers and
chaplains; and the academic element of the junior command
and staff course for new captains.

The Academy's commissioning course lasts 44 weeks, with
all intakes entering as officer cadets. The system of a separate
course for graduates has long been abolished, mainly in the
hope of removing the internal rivalry that once dogged
Sandhurst, between graduates and officer cadets with only
A Levels. Today all new cadets can expect to start as
probationary second lieutenants, but even with the shake-up

57

in courses, there is still jealousy between the two factions. Many non-graduate cadets accuse the Army of unnecessarily pampering the graduates and most feel that those officers with degrees – 50 per cent of all serving officers – are promoted more quickly than other members of their intake. However, the Army puts the frequent but not automatic rapid promotion of graduates down to their seniority; most are in their early to mid-twenties and often have more than four years' experience of living away from home. Naturally, this tends to make them more mature and independent. But some Sandhurst permanent staff argue that many graduates are less committed than non-graduates and more intent on their own prospects, which results in a higher proportion of graduate drop-outs compared to the rest of the course.

Women now complete the same training schedule as men at the Academy, which can add some humour to a stressful programme. Initial fears of a lowering of standards have not been justified.

Though women are not expected to lead men into battle, they still have to complete the Combat Tactics and Counter-Revolutionary Warfare lectures. Female officer cadets, once under some chauvinistic pressure from their male counter-parts, now have universal acceptance, resulting largely from the Gulf War and the part female officers played in many battle-group and brigade headquarters. Their calmness was demonstrated by their ability to make snap, but correct, decisions when confronted with an often confused and heated engagement during battle. A feminine input is now considered a valuable asset to any regiment, and many male officers who once resented their presence now welcome them with open arms.

The commissioning course is designed to develop the leadership potential the cadets displayed during their RCB and also to prepare them to be competent troop and platoon commanders. A common saying among the directing staff is that leaders are not born but create themselves through hard work.

The permanent staff at Sandhurst has gradually been changed from the mixed bag derived from many different regiments, to mainly officers and senior NCOs from the Guards and Light Infantry. Cadets are divided into companies on arrival. Each company is commanded by a major, with a captain as second-in-command. The basic teaching unit is the platoon, comprising up to 30 cadets of mixed commissions. Each platoon has a captain instructor, but much of the training is carried out by a colour sergeant or staff sergeant. The cadets are always called 'Sir', albeit with a capital 'C'!

The most prestigious other ranks appointment at Sandhurst is that of Academy Sergeant-Major, which always commands the correct pronunciation of 'Sir'. Being the most senior warrant officer in the British Army, he normally stays at the Academy for ten years before retiring at the age of 55. His preference for a non-commissioned rank rather than accept a late-entry commission and promotion to Major can be understood when taken in context. After all, there are plenty of majors in the Army but only one Academy Sergeant-Major, and the extent of his power is awesome.

Having such a figure has certainly helped to remove the old 'sausage machine' syndrome of all officers passing out of Sandhurst as clones. Today's officers are taught self-discipline, the ability to work under pressure, and strength of mind.

The cadets' day starts at 6 a.m. and ends after midnight, but they are rarely aware of time in the buzz of activity at the Academy. The stamping and slapping of boots and rifles from the drill-square combines with the shrill cries of warrant officers doubling platoons from skill at arms to the gym for a 'beasting'. The cadets move from one lecture to another in a blurred haze. The diversity of subjects covered is bewildering. War studies, military law, the Geneva Convention, tactics and history are shadowed by kit inspections, assault courses, initiative tests, weapons training, night navigation and battlecraft exercises, all designed to induce stress and cause a shock to the system.

Military exercises on Salisbury Plain are cold, wet and miserable, but the cadets attack each task with dogged determination. It is reiterated constantly that soldiers will rely on them for the correct battlefield tactics, enemy vehicle recognition, training programmes and fitness, but more importantly that they must lead their men fearlessly from the front.

The officer cadets' physical fitness training sessions are much harsher than those of the basic recruit. Forced marches are followed by the assault course or a session of command tasks. The weekly ritual of the 3-mile log race is met with agonised and exhausted faces; the 30-ft log has to be carried by sections of eight cadets over undulating, arduous terrain and through streams, mud and eerie, silent forests. The cadets are punished for bad performances with webbing runs and extra long gym sessions. The lazy or slow are made to carry a section of a tank track around the accommodation block until they are told to stop; the habit of the permanent staff 'forgetting' the cadet has now ended but for most officers it is still an experience that seems to last for ever.

The worst physical test for the young cadets is the assault, march and shoot. On a wet, windy, grassy plain the potential officers, dressed in full battle order with muddy helmets, rifles and webbing, stand doubled over, shaking, coughing and wheezing. Behind them, the last remaining cadets scramble up nets and over 12-ft walls, with cuts and bloody noses, while others wade through streams and slip down wet ropes. All around, PTIs sarcastically mock them: 'Come on now, Sir. Don't be scared! It's only water!'

The tired and flustered cadets are then formed up and double away on the long forced march to the firing range; every mile or so they slow to a brisk walk, but before they have time to catch their breath, they are off at the double again. The route takes deceiving twists, towards then away from the warmth and comfort of the accommodation blocks. The rain pours down and soaks them, and as the firing ranges come into sight, the relief is self-evident as cadets close their eyes and whisper prayers of thanks.

The crack of SA80s drowns out the groans of pain and cramp; bullets hit the Figure 11 targets and disappear in a cloud of wet sand behind. Accuracy is not important but speed is; each cadet lets loose the quota of rounds and doubles to the waiting trucks and protection from the severe weather. Few words are spoken as they are bounced and bumped around in the four-tonners on their way back to camp; many are too preoccupied with protecting their bruised and battered bodies from the pain.

The officer cadets complete a Counter Revolutionary Warfare syllabus, which includes the 'Troubles' in Northern Ireland, as they have become known. They spend a week doing FIBUA training (Fighting In a Built-Up Area) at a disused married quarters complex. The mock streets painted with anti-British slogans certainly look like Northern Ireland, but the civilians and terrorists are volunteer soldiers from local regiments who enjoy the opportunity to 'give the Ruperts some stick'. Here the cadets will carry out a basic standard of training, including suspect vehicle checkpoints, patrolling, house-clearance drills and mock cordons and searches. So far during the commissioning course, the cadets have learned how to command troops in conventional warfare, but this training gives them the chance to experience unconventional or guerrilla warfare. More intensive and specialised training is carried out with the Northern Ireland Training Advisory Teams, one in England for UK-based forces and the other in Germany for troops from the Mobile Reaction Force destined for service in the Province. This more in-depth training covers everything from riot control, body searching, prison escapes and street patrolling to the procedures for securing evidence and 'bagging' suspects – putting plastic bags on their hands to prevent the removal of forensic evidence. Officers are then able to conduct urban and rural operations anywhere within the Province.

When a contact is reported, whether a suspect bomb, a rocket attack or a shooting, the officer can call upon a multitude of specialised teams, including the Royal Logistics Corps bomb disposal teams, the Royal Engineers special search teams or the Army Air Corps helicopters for evacuation.

In spite of the frustrations and disappointments officers feel, they do enjoy a sense of satisfaction at the tours of duty. It gives them an opportunity to see their soldiers mature while the older soldiers revel in doing what they are best at, *soldiering*.

Etiquette

To the amusement of some Guards and Cavalry officers, the course now caters for those cadets who require 'etiquette' training. Some senior officers frown at the thought of having to teach young officers to be 'gentlemen'. 'Many years ago,' they say with disdain, 'officers could act no other way.' However, with a high proportion of officers coming from state schools or by promotion through the ranks, it is a sign of the times.

The cadets are taught to dress to a middle-class average and to look smart in both military and civilian attire. They learn that as an officer in Her Majesty's Army they will always be watched, whether by their men or by civilians attached to the barracks. These behaviour lessons, including such delights as mess procedure, after-dinner conversation and good manners, help the cadets to play the role expected of today's commissioned officers.

This new role can bring with it financial stress and potential impropriety, but many regimental commanding officers no longer stand for officer debt and, unlike junior ranks who only have to report loans, all officers must inform their superior of any current, or future, hire purchase agreements, regardless of the amount. Discretion and common sense play an important part of the commanding officer's appraisal, and if the officer is financially secure, there will be little investigation of his other affairs. Though many young subalterns suffer with the same financial pressures that many new soldiers face the problem is much more serious with junior ranks, but a soldier's need to 'fit in' and be accepted is more acute than within the officer ranks.

The Sovereign's Parade

The highlight of the commissioning course is the pass-out, commonly called the Sovereign's Parade. In good Army tradition, the passing-out cadets march from the parade ground, up the steps and past the pillars of the Grand Entrance of Old Building and down the long Victorian Corridor followed by the Adjutant on a grey charger. The cadets once received their commissions when the doors were clanged shut behind them, but after an embarrassing episode between a newly commissioned officer and a Sergeant-Major, when the young officer attempted to jail the senior NCO in retaliation for months of persecution, cadets now receive their commissions at midnight.

Later that day the cadets are officially 'dined in' at the Commissioning Ball, wearing their new regimental mess dress with the new pips covered until the midnight deadline, when wives and girlfriends remove the neatly tied bows and instantly promote the cadets into officers.

Some older officers regret the changes that have been forced on Sandhurst over the last few years. In its defence, the Academy staff point out that the overall standard has not been allowed to slip, but they also admit that a small percentage of officers who are substandard are allowed to pass through the system. However, they add with some force that these will be found out in the end. Those who do pass off are only as good or bad as their instructors, and although the system may have been changed, the standards have not.

When the newly commissioned officers arrive at their regiments as 21-year-old lieutenants, they will be given command of a rifle platoon, or some similar post in the non-infantry arms. Their careers will then be split between regimental posts and outside staff work, and most officers can expect to spend at least six years of their careers on a variety of courses, many of which will be held at Sandhurst. Their regiments will train and develop them for a variety of duties within the Army and later for senior commands within NATO, and the young subalterns are expected to stay in touch with national and international current affairs.

Normally an officer's career begins to take off at 26 with promotion to Captain and successful completion of the Junior Division of the Staff College at Warminster. 'High flyers' can expect further promotion after passing the harder examination for promotion from Captain to Major at 29. Promotion to higher posts is based on confidential reports, which all officers read and sign. To rise to the highest level, they must obtain at least four 'outstandings', which is very rare indeed, or be adjudged 'excellent', with the recommendation 'yes, now' for each additional promotion. If they receive just one 'yes, in his turn' their climb to the top will be slowed dramatically, although not permanently. Whether promotion is fast in coming or not, the fact remains that it is vitally important that all officers, at whatever level, should strive for perfection throughout their careers. Because, quite simply, lives depend upon it.

CHAPTER 7

Arms and the Corps

'Keep your hands off the regiments, you icono-
clastic civilians who meddle and muddle in Army
matters: you are not soldiers and you do not
understand them.'
Field Marshal Viscount Wolseley, 1903

In July 1990, the Government's 'Options for Change' review
announced a fundamental restructuring of Britain's armed
forces in the light of changing international circumstances.
The main objective was a smaller, better-equipped force that
would be properly trained, housed and motivated.

Inevitably, given the scale of the cuts, there were winners
and losers, and the Army suffered the biggest reductions.
Many famous and not so famous regiments were disbanded
or amalgamated. The Infantry and the Royal Armoured
Corps were the worst affected; the Armoured Corps lost seven
regiments and the Infantry 19 through amalgamations, and a
further nine battalions were disbanded. The only regiment that
remained totally unchanged by the review, not surprisingly,
was the Special Air Service.

The British Army in Germany became the first casualty of
the reductions. The British Army of the Rhine was reduced
from three armoured brigades to one, with a loss of over
27,000 service personnel. To the dismay of many outsiders,
the 'heavy' Army in Germany, as it was known, had been
totally demolished.

Regiments in England also fared badly. Although figures had always been fudged, regiments found themselves
having to reduce their staffing levels much further than
expected, so much so that some commanding officers in
the Royal Armoured Corps felt they would be unable to
stay operational.

While the MoD was trying desperately to introduce a new
management strategy to cope with the increasing number of

64

amalgamations and disbandments, it also had to implement a fundamental reorganisation and restructuring of the Army's logistical corps, a task it was finding increasingly problematic. Almost inevitably, overworked staff were going to make mistakes. The worst concerned two regiments that were moved from bases in Germany to the UK, only to find there was a shortage of permanent accommodation. It later emerged that this was due to an oversight by an MoD department which had authorised the return of accommodation blocks to the local authorities without informing the Army's housing staff. The troops had to be housed in temporary quarters until the problem was solved. Soon after this incident the Government announced a review of the MoD in a new defence cost study, and soon after the 'Front Line First' proposals were announced in late 1994, the department concerned was closed down.

Nevertheless, although the Army went through a lot of turmoil, it has now emerged as a smaller and better-equipped force. Whether this will be enough to withstand the challenges that the new world order will bring, only time will tell.

The Army is made up of regiments and corps, each of which has a vital and specific military function. As we have seen, these regiments and corps are divided between the Combat Arms and the Services. Combat Arm regiments are those that are deployed to front-line battlefield positions or support front-line regiments directly with fire support weaponry, like the Artillery or Army Air Corps. The Services are made up of attachments of logistics troops who, though they have a war footing and are also trained in fighting skills, have the additional responsibility of resupplying the combat troops.

In this chapter I discuss the history, the entry requirements, the personal characteristics needed, the working environment, the future opportunities and the postings of every regiment and corps in the Army, with the exception of the Army Legal Service Branch, the Royal Army Chaplains' Department and the Royal Gurkha Rifles. These have deliberately been omitted, mainly because the specialist nature of their work and limited recruitment opportunities make them unavailable to most candidates.

The Household Division

The Household Division is the senior formation in the Army, and consists of two regiments of the Household Cavalry and five regiments of Foot Guards. These soldiers, with their scarlet uniforms and tall bearskins or silver helmets, have become the most famous ceremonial troops in the world. All but the Irish and Welsh Guards have pedigrees dating back to the time of the Civil War in the seventeenth century and the restoration of the monarchy that followed it.

The Household Division recruits nationally on principle, so that all parts of the United Kingdom have the opportunity to guard their Sovereign. Some Guards regiments actively seek to recruit from home bases first, but others are not so fussy – so much so, that within the Scots Guards there is a higher ratio of 'Geordies' than 'Jocks'.

The Household Cavalry

Although the Household Cavalry is a separate formation from other armoured cavalry regiments, it carries out similar work on the battlefield. The difference is that it has the more prestigious task of guarding the sovereign. Consisting of the Life Guards and the Blues and Royals, between them they provide an armoured reconnaissance regiment and the mounted regiment in London.

HISTORY   Both regiments were formed in 1660 and are among the oldest in the Army. The Life Guards were first named the Horse Guards and were used to escort Charles II to London from exile in Belgium; they were renamed the Horse Grenadier Guards in 1678 and split in 1788 to form the 1st and 2nd Regiments of Life Guards. These regiments were later amalgamated to form the current regiment. The Blues and Royals were formed in 1660 as the Royal Regiment of Horse Guards and renamed the Royal Horse Guards (Blues) in 1746; they became part of the Household Division in 1821. Today's regiment was created by the amalgamation of the Royal Horse Guards and the Royal Dragoons in 1969. Both regiments have played an active part in maintaining the monarchy over the last three centuries, and have seen active service in nearly every part of the world.

PERSONAL CHARACTERISTICS   Soldiers need to be of above average intelligence. Physical fitness and stamina are essential as the days are long and tiring; a love for horses is also required for those destined for ceremonial duties. Soldiers need to be able to work in a team and be prepared to spend many months away from family and friends.

WORKING CONDITIONS   Soldiers on ceremonial duties start the day at 0630 and are on the roads with the horses by 0700; returning to feed their mounts by 0830. Troopers then clean and groom all the horses. The rest of the day consists of practising drill and looking after the horses. Soldiers can also expect to be given night duty watching the horses. Life in the Household Cavalry armoured reconnaissance regiment is the same as in the Royal Armoured Corps.

ENTRY REQUIREMENTS   No formal qualifications needed.

POSTINGS   The Blues and Royals are currently completing ceremonial duties in London and The Life Guards are the armoured reconnaissance regiment in Windsor. Soldiers destined for the latter can expect training in the UK, Germany and Canada, with six-month UN duties in Cyprus. Soldiers are normally posted to ceremonial duties for three years after passing off.

The Foot Guards

It is difficult to pick out the individual regiments of the Foot Guards on public parade. One method of identification is by the groupings of their tunic buttons; each is arranged differently depending upon seniority. The Grenadiers' buttons are spaced evenly in ones; the Coldstreams' in sets of two; the Scots Guards' in threes; the Irish in fours and the Welsh Guards' in fives.

HISTORY   The attitude of the Guards to their special position in the Army is somewhat mixed. Although they enjoy the glamour of state occasions and take great pride in their links with the monarchy, they resent any suggestion that they are 'toy soldiers' put on parade to look pretty but quickly replaced when the real fighting starts. They are in fact real soldiers, as they have proved throughout their history and more recently during the Falklands Campaign.

The question of seniority is important within the Guards. The Coldstream Guards, for example, refuse to march directly behind the Grenadiers and prefer to bring up the rear, an ancient right bestowed on the second most senior regiment in the Army.

PERSONAL CHARACTERISTICS   A guardsman needs to be versatile and quick-thinking. He must be prepared to work as part of a team, and be physically fit.

WORKING CONDITIONS   Ceremonial duties consist of a day on followed by two days off guard duty, broken down into two-hour shifts or 'stags', followed by four hours off. Away from ceremonial duties, soldiers normally spend their time preparing for the following day's duty or sleeping. Weekend leave is rare. Guardsmen posted to mechanised battalions spend most of their time working as normal infantry soldiers.

ENTRY REQUIREMENTS   No formal qualifications needed.

POSTINGS   Soldiers can expect postings to bases within the UK for ceremonial duties, to Germany and Canada for infantry exercises, on peace-keeping duties in Cyprus and Bosnia and operational service in Northern Ireland.

The Grenadier Guards
HISTORY   Today's regiment was raised at Bruges when Charles II was in exile, and was named the Wentworth's Foot Guards. They were renamed Russell's Foot Guards in 1660 and then changed to the 1st Grenadier Regiment of Foot Guards. The most senior company in the regiment has the honour of being the Sovereign's Own Company, and provides the guard at coronations and state funerals, a tradition that dates back to Charles II.

The Coldstream Guards
HISTORY   Formed in 1650 as Monck's Regiment of Foot, this is the only regiment in the Army with a lineal descent from

the Parliamentary Army of the Protectorate. They entered the King's service as the Lord General's Regiment of Foot Guards, and were given their current name in 1670. Their first battle honour was awarded at Tangier in 1680 and the regiment also holds the honour of Lincelles, only awarded to three other regiments. The motto is *Nulli Secundus* ('Second to none').

The Scots Guards
HISTORY The regiment was raised in 1641 by the King's warrant as the Argyll's, and renamed in 1650 the Foot Regiment of His Majesty's Life Guard; this regiment was disbanded in 1651 and many of its officers and ranks went on to form the first company of Foot Guards in 1661. The regiment's first recorded action was in 1666 at Rullion Green and they were added to the 'English Establishment' soon after.

Dating the regiment back to 1641 makes it the oldest in the Foot Guards, but this carries very little weight in the Household Division. More recently the Scots Guards were actively involved in the recapture of the Falkland Islands; not only did they shoot down the aircraft that bombed the support ships *Sir Galahad* and *Sir Tristram*, but in hand-to-hand fighting they also captured Mount Tumbledown in a decisive action that led to the cease-fire. After hostilities ended they remained in position in the Falklands for some time, and were the last battalion to return home.

The Irish Guards
HISTORY Raised by an Army order at the behest of Queen Victoria to commemorate the bravery shown by her Irish regiments in the Boer War, the regiment's first honour was recorded in 1914 at the retreat from Mons, Marne. Today it has completed tours in Northern Ireland, Cyprus and the Falklands. Its regimental motto is *Quis Separabit* ('Who shall separate').

The Welsh Guards
HISTORY Raised in 1915 by a royal warrant from the king, this is the youngest and least senior regiment of the Foot Guards. Their first battle honour was in 1916 at the Somme. The regiment has completed tours in Northern

Ireland and Hong Kong. The motto is *Cymru am Byth* ('Wales for ever').

The Royal Artillery

Royal Horse Artillery and
the Royal Regiments of Artillery

HISTORY   Formed in 1716 with two companies, and later grouped with the Gibraltar and Minorca companies to form today's Royal Regiment of Artillery. Artillery is the oldest form of long-range firepower in the world. It has been used since ancient times, when soldiers used catapults to throw rocks at siege fortifications. The old French principle that the artillery conquered while the infantry occupied, is as true today as it was in Napoleon's time. The Royal Artillery is the only regiment not to display battle honours; its widespread service in all theatres of war is represented simply with the motto *Ubique* (Everywhere).

It is split into two components, the Royal Regiment of Artillery and the Royal Horse Artillery (RHA). The RHA has a much higher standard of presentation than their Royal Regiment counterparts. Artillery officers spend three years with the RHA before moving back to the Royal Regiment, which has the effect of raising the standards of the Artillery as a whole.

The Royal Artillery has 16 regiments with individual tasks on today's battlefield. The Royal Horse Artillery was formed in 1945 on the orders of King George VI and named the Riding Troop, RHA. It was renamed the King's Troop, RHA, two years later.

Although the Royal Horse Artillery ranks second in precedence to the Household Cavalry, it would in fact, if the Army was to parade in its entirety, take the right of the line and have precedence over all other regiments and corps, including the Household Cavalry.

PERSONAL CHARACTERISTICS   Soldiers need to be articulate, unexcitable, and physically fit. They must be prepared to work in combat conditions and have technical and practical skills experience.

WORKING CONDITIONS   These are often dirty and smelly.

Soldiers work in oily, greasy and muddy engine compartments, both in camp and on exercise. While on exercise crews live in small confined spaces, with little or no room to move. This corps is not recommended for the claustrophobic.

ENTRY REQUIREMENTS   On the whole no formal qualifications needed, but for some of the more technical trades a minimum of three GCSEs in mathematics, English and a science subject are required.

POSTINGS   Artillery soldiers can be posted anywhere in the world, but first postings are normally to a regiment based in Germany.

The Royal Armoured Corps

HISTORY   The cavalry regiments of the Armoured Corps date back to the seventeenth century, and with the invention of the tank during the First World War there was fierce competition between the regiments to be the first to be equipped, a phenomenon that has continued to this day. The Royal Armoured Corps was formed in 1939 and is divided into the old cavalry of the line and the new royal tank regiments, considered by the former to be a little too serious. The role of these regiments is as either armoured or armoured reconnaissance units. The armoured regiments are equipped with the main battle tank, the Challenger 1, which is due to be replaced by the Challenger 2 by the end of the century.

PERSONAL CHARACTERISTICS   Soldiers have to be sharp, articulate, hard-working and prepared to live and work in cramped conditions. They need a high degree of self-discipline and perseverance, must be prepared to work as part of a team of four, and have a good sense of humour.

WORKING CONDITIONS   As for the Royal Artillery.

ENTRY REQUIREMENTS   No formal qualifications needed.

POSTINGS   Soldiers can often spend more than ten years in one posting. Service as the UN peace-keeping force in Cyprus comes around once every six years and service in Northern Ireland is rare. Regiments also undertake training exercises in Canada every two years.

1st Queen's Dragoon Guards
HISTORY   Formed in 1959 from the 1st King's Dragoon Guards and the Queen's Bays, both dating back to 1685, the regiment's first battle honour was recorded at Blenheim. It remained unchanged in the current round of amalgamation. It did not take part in the Gulf War, but has recently completed tours of Northern Ireland and Canada. The regiment's motto is *Pro Rege et Patria* ('For king and country').

The Royal Scots Dragoon Guards (*Carabiniers and Greys*)
HISTORY   Formed in 1971 from the Royal Scots Greys and the 3rd Carabiniers. The Carabiniers were formed in 1922 from two English regiments raised in 1685, the 3rd (Prince of Wales) Dragoon Guards and the 6th Dragoon Guards (Carabiniers). The Royal Scots Greys originated from the Royal Regiment of Scots Dragoons in 1681. Although the Scots Greys were formed four years earlier as 'dragoons', they took precedence after the Carabiniers. Both regiments enjoyed a formidable reputation on the battlefield and were the most feared of all the cavalry regiments. The motto is *Nemo Me Impune Lacessit* ('No one provokes me with impunity'). The new armoured regiment has recently returned from live-firing exercises in Canada.

The Queen's Royal Lancers
HISTORY   Formed after the amalgamation of the 16/5th Queen's Royal Hussars and the 17/21st Lancers on 25 June 1993. The 16/5th was created in 1922 by the merger of the 5th (Royal Irish) Lancers and the 16th (The Queen's) Lancers. The 17/21st was formed by the 1922 amalgamation of the 17th Lancers (Duke of Cambridge's Own), who led the charge of the Light Brigade, and the 21st Lancers (The Empress of India's). More recently the 16/5th provided the 1st Armoured Division's forward reconnaissance screen during the Gulf War.

9/12th Royal Hussars (*Prince of Wales's*)
HISTORY   Unchanged in the recent amalgamations but formed in 1960 from the 9th (Queen's Royal Lancers) and the 12th

Royal Lancers (Prince of Wales's Own). The officers in the regiment still sing five hymns after formal occasions, as a tradition marking the penance imposed for raiding a monastery during the Peninsula War. The regiment's motto is *Honi Soit Qui Mal y Pense* ('Evil to him who thinks evil'). Battle honours include such famous names as Salamanca, Waterloo, the Somme and Dunkirk.

Royal Dragoon Guards
HISTORY   Formed on 1 August 1992 with the amalgamation of the 4/7th Royal Dragoon Guards and the 5th Royal Inniskilling Dragoon Guards. The 4/7th was formed in 1922 by the merger of the 4th (Royal Hussars) Dragoon Guards and the 7th (Princess Royal's) Dragoon Guards, and the 5th was also formed in 1922 by the amalgamation of the 5th (Princess of Wales's) Dragoon Guards and the 6th or Inniskilling Dragoons. Both regiments were honoured at Blenheim.

The Dragoons saw their first action in 1678, when three troops were formed to break up illegal gatherings of the Covenanters. More recently the regiment have been involved in the Gulf War and Bosnia.

The Light Dragoons
HISTORY   Formed after the amalgamation of the 13/18th Royal Hussars (Queen Mary's Own) and the 15/19th King's Royal Hussars on 1 December 1992. The 13/18th was formed by the amalgamation in 1922 of the 13th Hussars and the 18th Royal Hussars (Queen Mary's Own). The 15/19th was also created in 1922 by the merger of the 15th (The King's) Hussars and the 19th (Queen Alexandra's Own Royal) Hussars. Neither regiment was involved in the Gulf War, but the new regiment has recently seen service in Bosnia.

The King's Royal Hussars
HISTORY   Formed after the amalgamation of the 14/20th King's Hussars and the Royal Hussars (Prince of Wales's Own), which was itself created from the 10th (Prince of Wales's Royal) Hussars and the 11th Prince Albert's Own Hussars. The 14/20th were formed in 1922 from the 14th (King's) Hussars and the 2nd Bengal Cavalry, converted to the 20th Hussars. Today the regiment still maintains the

tradition, from the 11th Hussars, of sounding the last post at 2150, the time of Lord Cardigan's death. The 14/20th had a successful Gulf War and won much praise for its dogged determination and fighting efficiency under enemy fire.

The Queen's Royal Hussars
(The Queen's Own and Royal Irish)
HISTORY Formed after the amalgamation of the Queen's Own Hussars and the Queen's Royal Irish Hussars in 1993, the QOH was created after the amalgamation in 1958 from the 3rd (King's Own) Hussars and the 7th (Queen's Own) Hussars.

During the Battle of Dettingen in 1743, the regimental guidon was captured by a French cavalry unit. In a remarkable act of bravery, Trooper Thomas Brown, alone and armed with only a short cutlass, commandeered a horse and chased, captured and killed the cavalry party before returning the prized guidon back to regimental lines. During his courageous act, he not only received several near fatal wounds to his head, face and body but also lost three fingers and was shot in the back twice. King George II, upon hearing the story, rode to the regiment's encampment where he revived the tradition of the knight's banneret and bestowed the honour on the young trooper. Brown was the first and last non-commissioned soldier in history to be awarded such an honour on the field of battle.

The QRIH was formed by the amalgamation of the 4th (Queen's Own) Hussars and the 8th (King's Royal Irish) Hussars. The silver scarlet Maid of Warsaw arm badge is worn on the left sleeve by every soldier in the regiment. It was awarded to the 7th Hussars by the commander of the 2nd Polish Corps, in recognition of their valour in supporting the Poles throughout the Italian campaign in 1944–5. Although the QOH was not involved in the Gulf War, the QRIH was, and like the 14/20th King's Hussars received praise for its superior fighting prowess and professionalism.

The 1st and 2nd Royal Tank Regiments
HISTORY The 1st RTR was formed by the amalgamation of the 1st and 4th RTR regiments in 1994 and the 2nd RTR was created by the merger of the 2nd and 3rd RTR, also in 1994.

The RTR regiments were formed in 1916 as a heavy section of the Machine Gun Corps, and changed a year later to the Tank Corps. The current name was adopted in 1935. The Corps' first battle honour was awarded in 1916 at the Battle of the Somme.

The soldiers stay with one of the two regiments, while the officers switch between them on their climb up the promotion ladder.

The RTRs like to think of themselves as the Armoured Corps' 'paratroopers', but with black berets.

The Royal Corps of Signals

HISTORY The Royal Signals was formed during World War Two and has remained unchanged. Yet the Corps' communications technology has developed greatly since then; no longer do military commanders rely on short-range radio or the carrier pigeon. Today's communications system is the most advanced in the world, using voice and data transmissions and satellite communications. In addition, the Royal Signals wage electronic warfare (eavesdropping on enemy transmitters) while disguising their own electronic signature. The Corps' motto is *Certa Cito* ('Swift and Sure').

PERSONAL CHARACTERISTICS Soldiers need to be hard workers, with mental agility and initiative. There is a high need for soldiers to have technical skills and be able to work alone. The Royal Signals is a 'corporal's corps' – soldiers and NCOs must take responsibility when officers are not available, especially in remote postings like the Falklands or Ascension Island.

WORKING CONDITIONS Most work is in clean, well-lit workshops. Exercises are frequent. Soldiers need to be able to spend long hours alone when on special duties, like rebroadcast stations.

ENTRY REQUIREMENTS Most employments need a minimum of three GCSEs at Grades A–C.

POSTINGS Soldiers can be posted anywhere in the world and change postings every two years.

The Royal Engineers

HISTORY   The Royal Engineers help to form the framework of the modern battlefield; their task is to deny areas to the enemy and force them into 'killing zones'. Today military engineering has advanced in line with the rest of the Army. Mine-laying that once took 16 hours and 25 soldiers to cover a 1,000-yard area now takes ten minutes and the press of a button.

PERSONAL CHARACTERISTICS   Soldiers need above all to be physically fit and prepared for hard work, as being a combat engineer is a dirty and thankless job.

WORKING CONDITIONS   Soldiers can expect to work on many given tasks. Work is often dirty and smelly and exercises can be long and hard. Soldiers can specialise in one area of engineering after three years.

ENTRY REQUIREMENTS   No formal qualifications needed.

POSTINGS   World-wide, but normally the first posting is to a German- or UK-based regiment.

The Infantry

HISTORY   The infantry accounts for a quarter of the Army and bears the brunt of any fighting. It acts as a peace-keeping force both in Britain and overseas, and although the term 'line infantry' gives the impression of uniformity, the reality is just the opposite; every regiment has its own traditions and loyalties, and guards them jealously.

PERSONAL CHARACTERISTICS   Soldiers must be able to follow orders without question, be prepared to make decisions quickly and accept responsibility. They need a high degree of physical fitness and stamina, plus a sense of humour.

WORKING CONDITIONS   Infantry soldiers spend much of their time preparing for overseas operations and war. Much time is given to practising skills on exercise and low-intensity operations. Soldiers move between lectures and practical training sessions in and out of barracks.

ENTRY REQUIREMENTS No formal qualifications needed.

POSTINGS Infantry soldiers can be posted to any part of the world, including Germany, Cyprus, Canada, Northern Ireland, Bosnia and the Falkland Islands.

The Royal Scots (*The Royal Regiment*)
HISTORY Formed in 1633 as Sir John Hepburn's Regiment, and changed to the Royal Regiment of Foot in 1684, this is the oldest regiment in the Army, with the longest record of continuous service. It was renamed the Royal Scots Regiment before being given their current name in 1920. The first battle honour was awarded at Tangier in 1680, but more recently the regiment has completed tours in Germany, Northern Ireland and Cyprus. The service the Royal Scots have given the British crown over the last 350 years is illustrated by the impressive list of battle honours.

The Princess of Wales's Royal Regiment
HISTORY Formed after the amalgamation of the Queen's Regiment and the Royal Hampshire Regiment in 1992. The Queen's Regiment was formed in 1966 by the amalgamation of four home-counties regiments: The Queen's Royal Surreys (the old Second of Foot), the Queen's Own Buffs (the Third of Foot) and the Royal Sussex and Middlesex Regiments. Officers of the 2nd Battalion are allowed to drink the loyal toast sitting down, a legacy dating back to 1702 when the regiment spent days as marines on board ships of the line. The Royal Hampshire Regiment was formed in 1881 by the amalgamation of the 37th and 67th, North and South Hampshire Regiments respectively. Known as the Tigers, a nickname given them by George IV, the regiment was unchanged in the amalgamations of the 1960s. It was one of the first regiments deployed to Northern Ireland when the troubles began in 1969.

The King's Own Royal Border Regiment
HISTORY Formed in 1959 from the King's Own Royal Lancaster Regiment and the Border Regiment. Both regiments dated back to 1680, when they were formed as the 2nd Tangier Regiment. The first battle honour was awarded at Namur in 1695. This regiment also drinks the loyal toast seated. Its

77

main recruitment area is Liverpool and Manchester, although soldiers are also drawn from other areas.

The Royal Regiment of Fusiliers

HISTORY   Although the Royal Regiment of Fusiliers remained unchanged in the latest round of cuts, they were not so lucky in 1968, when the current regiment was created by the amalgamation of four fusilier regiments: the Royal Northumberland Fusiliers, the Royal Warwickshire Fusiliers, the Royal Fusiliers and the Lancashire Fusiliers. The regional contrasts could not have been greater, but it did widen the pool from which potential soldiers could be recruited. The official mascot is an Indian black buck. The regiment's worst moment came when six of its soldiers were killed during the Gulf War, when an American A10 aircraft attacked two Warrior infantry fighting vehicles with its depleted uranium Gatling gun.

The King's Regiment

HISTORY   Formed in 1958 with the amalgamation of the King's Regiment (Liverpool) and the Manchester Regiment, both dating back to 1685, when Princess Anne of Denmark's Regiment was raised. The principal battle honour, Blenheim, records the regiment's heaviest loss in battle, where even though outnumbered, it stopped the French from escaping and captured over 1,000 prisoners. The regiment has completed tours in Hong Kong, Northern Ireland and Bosnia. The regimental motto is *Nec Aspera Terrent* ('Nor do difficulties deter').

The Royal Anglian Regiment

HISTORY   Formed in 1964 from the Royal Leicestershire and three East Anglian regiments, the 1st East Anglians (Royal Norfolk and Suffolk), the 2nd East Anglian (Duchess of Gloucester's Own Royal Lincolnshire and Northamptonshire) and the 3rd East Anglian (16/44th Foot). Each battalion has its own nickname; the first are the 'Vikings' and the second the 'Poachers'.

The Devonshire and Dorset Regiment

HISTORY   Formed in 1958 from the Devonshire and Dorset regiments. Both regiments date back to 1685, when the Duke

of Beaufort's Musketeers was created. They are known as
both the 'Janners' (the West Country version of 'John'), and
the 'Armoured Farmers', after they were mechanised during
the Second World War. The regiment still celebrates Clive's
Victory at Palas in 1755, where 300 men from the 39th, together
with 2,000 native troops, defeated an enemy force of 50,000. A
silver-headed drum major's staff presented at the time is still
kept in the Dorset Military Museum. Regimental mottos are
Semper Fidelis ('Ever faithful'), and *Primus in Indis* ('First in
India').

The Light Infantry
HISTORY   Formed from four former light infantry regiments,
the Somerset and Cornwall, the King's Own Yorkshire, the
King's Shropshire and the Durham, this regiment is famous
for its rapid drill and marching speeds, both on parade and
across country. The regiments date back to 1685, when they
were formed as the Earl of Huntingdon's Regiment and later
the 13th Foot. The first battle honour was at Gibraltar in
1704–5. Nieuport commemorates the gallant defence of that
town by the 53rd Regiment in 1793, when the garrison won
acclaim for its tenacious stand in holding off a besieging force
of 12,000 French troops for ten days. Today the Light Infantry
completes regular tours to Northern Ireland, Canada, America
and Germany. Regimental mottos include *Aucto Spendore
Resurgo* ('I rise again with greater splendour') and *Cede
Nullis* ('Yield to none').

The Prince of Wales's Own Regiment of Yorkshire
HISTORY   Formed in 1958 from the Prince of Wales's Own
(West Yorkshire) Regiment and the East Yorkshire Regiment
(Duke of York's Own). Both regiments date back to 1685.
They are predictably nicknamed the 'Yorkies', and have little
difficulty in recruiting new blood. The regiment was the first
to be deployed to Northern Ireland and more recently they
provided a large contingent of soldiers to guard Iraqi prisoners
and acted as the 1st Armoured Division's defence platoon
during the Gulf War.

The Green Howards
HISTORY   This is one of the few regiments never to have suffered amalgamation. Formed in 1688 as Luttrell's Regiment,

it changed names several times before being given its current name in 1920. Its first battle honour was awarded at Blenheim and it has strong links with the Norwegian royal family. It has little trouble recruiting from the North Yorkshire area.

Royal Highland Fusiliers (Princess Margaret's Own Glasgow and Ayrshire Regiment)

HISTORY   Formed after the amalgamation of the Royal Scots Fusiliers and the Highland Light Infantry in 1959. Both regiments date back to 1678 when they were formed as the Earl of Mar's Regiment. The first recorded battle honour was at Blenheim, although the regiments were involved in smaller skirmishes before that time. The Highland Light Infantry was the only regiment in the history of the British Army to have had all its officers killed or wounded in battle – at the Battle of Assaye in 1803. It was finally commanded by a quartermaster, a warrant officer class 1 at that time. Recently the regiment has completed tours in Northern Ireland and Bosnia.

The Cheshire Regiment

HISTORY   This is another regiment to have avoided amalgamation. It can trace its origins back to 1689 when it was formed as the Duke of Norfolk's Regiment. This name changed in 1782 to the 22nd (Cheshire) Regiment, and to its current name in 1881. The first battle honour was awarded at Louisburg, and the regiment was nicknamed 'the Red Knights' during the 1790s; recruitment was so poor that the 22nd resorted to enlisting boys from the poorhouse, and so that the officers could tell that they were illiterate, they were clothed in red. One of these orphans was later commissioned on the battlefield for his bravery. The regimental motto is *Ich Dien* ('I serve').

The Royal Welch Fusiliers

HISTORY   Formed in 1689 as the Lord Herbert's Regiment, the name was changed to the Royal Welsh Fusiliers in 1882 and to its current spelling in 1920. The Royal Welch has the oldest recorded example of a regimental mascot, the goat, dating back to 1775. Officers and guests do not stand for the National Anthem, a custom that has no solid origin, but which may date back to the time when the Prince Regent absolved them from the loyal toast because of the loyalty shown during the mutiny at the Nore in 1797.

The Royal Regiment of Wales (24th/41st Foot)

HISTORY   Formed in 1969 from the South Wales Borderers and the Welch Regiment, which date back to 1689 and 1719 respectively. The first battle honour was awarded at Blenheim. Recruitment is mainly from South Wales. The regimental motto is *Gwell Angau Na Chywilydd* ('Better death than dishonour').

The King's Own Scottish Borderers

HISTORY   Raised in 1689 as the Earl of Leven's or Edinburgh Regiment to protect the new Scottish monarchy, this regiment was renamed the King's Own Borderers in 1881 and took its current name in 1887. The first battle honour was awarded at Namur in 1695. Recently the regiment has returned from Bosnia, and its mottos are *In Veritate Religionis Confido* ('In the truth of religion I trust') and *Nisi Dominus Frustra* ('Unless the Lord be with us all is in vain').

The Royal Irish Regiment

HISTORY   Formed in 1968 from three regiments, the Royal Inniskilling Fusiliers, the Royal Ulster Rifles and the Royal Irish Fusiliers (Princess Victoria's). The regiment also uses its prefix the 27th (Inniskilling) 83rd and 87th, dating back to regiments from the sixteenth century. The first recorded battle honour was at Martinique in 1762. The Royal Ulster Rifles were given the nickname 'Stackies' because when on parade their dark green uniforms resembled a host of chimney stacks. The regimental motto is *Faugh-a-Ballagh* ('Clear the way').

The Royal Gloucestershire, Berkshire and Wiltshire Regiment

HISTORY   Created by the amalgamation of the Gloucestershire Regiment and the Duke of Edinburgh's Royal Regiment (Berkshire and Wiltshire) in early 1994. The Gloucestershire Regiment successfully beat off amalgamation in the 1960s, but the 'Duke's' did not; they were formed in 1959 from the Royal Berkshire Regiment (Princess Charlotte of Wales) and the Wiltshire Regiment (Duke of Edinburgh's). The

Gloucestershire Regiment was formed in 1694 as Gibson's Regiment and awarded its first battle honour at Rumillien. The 'Duke's' was originally raised from independent companies in Jamaica in 1744, and named Trawney's Regiment. Their first battle honour was awarded in 1778 at St Lucia. Recently, the regiment has served in Northern Ireland and Bosnia.

The Worcestershire and Sherwood Foresters (29/45th Foot)

HISTORY   Formed in 1970 by the amalgamation of the Worcestershire Regiment and the Sherwood Foresters (Derbyshire Regiment), which date back to 1694 and 1741 respectively. The regiment's first battle honour was at Ramillies. Its motto is simply, 'Firm'.

The Queen's Lancashire Regiment

HISTORY   Formed in 1970 from the Lancashire Regiment (Prince of Wales's Volunteers) and the Loyal North Lancashire Regiment. It dates back to 1702, when it was first raised as Sanderson's Marines. The first battle honour was awarded at Gibraltar in 1704–5. After the battle of Maida, Lieutenant Colonel Kempt made his supper from a tortoise and saved the shell as a memento; it was later mounted in silver as a snuff box and presented to the Officers' Mess. The regiment's main recruitment area is around Preston, Burnley and Blackburn, and although it went through a lean period during the mid-1980s, it is slowly increasing its recruitment figures to above the Army's average. The regimental motto is 'Loyally I serve'.

The Duke of Wellington's Regiment (West Riding)

HISTORY   Formed in 1702 as the Earl of Huntingdon's Regiment, and changed to the 33rd Duke of Wellington's Regiment in 1853, it amalgamated with the 76th in 1881 to form today's regiment. Its first recorded battle honour was at Dettingen, and it was once nicknamed the 'Old Immortals', a name which derives from the 76th's remarkable ability to return to strength after each devastating battle, which astounded Lord Lake at the time of the Mahratta Wars. Recently the regiment has completed tours in Northern Ireland, Bosnia and the Falklands. Its motto is *Virtutis Fortuna Comes* ('Fortune is the companion of bravery').

The Staffordshire Regiment (*The Prince of Wales's*)

HISTORY   Formed in 1959 from the North and South Staffordshire Regiments, which both date back to 1705, when Lillington's Regiment was created. The first battle honour was awarded at Guadaloupe in 1759. This is one of the few regiments which is able to get on with the Parachute Regiment, possibly because of its past Airborne history. It was one of the first regiments to be equipped with the Warrior and the first to deploy to the Gulf; as part of the 4th Armoured Brigade they saw a lot of action in the liberation of Kuwait.

The Black Watch

HISTORY   Today's regiment was raised after the 1715 rebellion to act as independent companies to 'watch' the Highlands. It was first called the 43rd or Highland Regiment, but this was officially changed to add the 'Black Watch' in 1881. Its first military action was in May 1745, when the Allied Army approached the French positions at Fontenoy, near Tournai. Though it was successful in capturing some enemy positions, it was ordered to withdraw after the French counter-attacked, but not before the Highlanders had fought with great bravery and determination, and earned the respect of their French foes.

The Highlanders (*Seaforth, Gordons and Camerons*)

HISTORY   Formed in September 1994 by the amalgamation of the Queen's Own Highlanders and the Gordon Highlanders. The Queen's Own Highlanders was an amalgamation of the 72nd and 78th Highland Regiments and the 79th Queen's Own Regiment, and saw its first action in 1779 when defending the Channel Islands against a French expeditionary force. The Gordon Highlanders were formed in 1881 from the 75th Stirlingshire and the 92nd Gordon Highlanders. Their first action was in 1790, when they stormed and captured Fort Choughaset in the Third Mysore War.

The Argyll and Sutherland Highlanders

HISTORY   Formed in 1881 by the amalgamation of the 91st Princess Louise's Argyllshire Highlanders and the 93rd (Sutherland) Highlanders, which date back to 1794 and 1799 respectively. The regiment's first battle honour was awarded to the 93rd at the Cape of Good Hope in 1806.

Today the regiment has completed tours in Northern Ireland and Bosnia. The regimental mottos are *Ne Obliviscaris* ('Do not forget'), and *Sans Peur* ('Without fear').

The Parachute Regiment

HISTORY   Winston Churchill wrote a famous memo in June 1940, calling on the Chiefs of Staff for 'at least 5,000 parachute troops'; nine days later the Central Landing School was set up at Ringway Airport near Manchester as the first British training camp. The 1st Parachute Battalion developed from No. 2 Commando, and the first operational raid took place on the Tragino Aqueduct in Italy in February 1942, with mixed results. The Parachute Regiment was not officially formed until August 1942. Until then it was part of the Army Air Corps. This was more an administrative move than an operational commitment, however, and the regiment regards June 1940 as the time when it all began.

It was given the nickname the 'Red Devils' by the German Army during the Second World War and, although it was never meant as a compliment, the name has stuck and is used by the regiment's free-fall parachute display team. Over 3,000 members of the regiment were killed and another 8,000 listed as missing in action during the war, which reflects the often hazardous operations they were involved in.

Since the war, the regiment, formed into three battalions, has seen service in many parts of the world, from Palestine to Belfast, the Far East to Suez, Cyprus, Borneo, Aden, the Falklands and more recently Rwanda.

Today, the regiment maintains one battalion in the parachute role at Aldershot, and the other two as infantry battalions. All battalions take their turn in Northern Ireland and in the parachute role, which means that each will only serve as the airborne unit for two years out of every six.

Selection is amongst the hardest in the Army, but ensures that only the best are accepted. The Parachute Regiment is normally deployed as Britain's first response to any hostilities. Airborne training calls for a great deal of strength and stamina, not to mention determination.

The Royal Green Jackets

HISTORY   The Royal Green Jackets were originally the old 'Ox and Bucks' Light Infantry, the King's Royal Rifle Corps (the 60th Rifles), and the Rifle Brigade, which date back to 1741 and 1755 respectively; the first battle honour was gained at Louisburg in 1758. Ranks are not used in the Officers' Mess and badges of rank are not worn. The only exception is the Colonel, who is addressed by his rank.

The Green Jackets have consistently produced more senior officers than any other part of the Army. During the Gulf War, two out of the four military members of the Army Board were Green Jackets and officers from the regiment are often promoted to influential positions. Whether this is due to the regiment's selection process or to senior officers 'looking after their own', it cannot be denied that it is an extremely successful regiment, and its officers are among the most talented in the Army.

Special Air Service Regiment

HISTORY   This famous regiment started life in the Western Desert in July 1941. It was founded by Lieutenant-Colonel David Stirling, a young officer in the Scots Guards, to carry out sabotage and intelligence missions behind enemy lines, a role that has remained unchanged to this day. The 1st and 2nd SAS Regiments were disbanded in 1945, but a territorial unit, 21 SAS (Artists) was re-formed in 1947. The 'Artist' refers to the Artists Rifles, a dashing and fashionable Territorial Army (TA) unit dating back to 1859. The '21' came about as a result of some complex reasoning. The original idea was to call it 12 SAS, incorporating the '1' and '2' of the 1st and 2nd Regiments, but this might have caused confusion with the existing 12th Airborne TA unit (now disbanded). So Army commanders reversed the figures and emerged with 21 SAS.

The current regular 22nd SAS Regiment was formed in Malaya in 1952, from the Malayan Scouts, which had been founded two years before to carry out SAS-type operations against Communist terrorists in the jungle, and seven years later the second TA unit was formed, 23 SAS.

Apart from the years 1960–3, the SAS has been engaged in active service continuously since 1952, including Malaya, Borneo, Aden, Oman, South Arabia, Northern Ireland, the Falklands, Afghanistan, the Gambia, Thailand, Cambodia, Liberia, Ethiopia, Bosnia, Haiti and the Gulf. Perhaps their most famous moment in the post-war years was on home soil, in London 1980, when black-clad figures abseiled down the walls of the Iranian Embassy in Princess Gate, to storm the building and rescue the 20 hostages being held by a fundamentalist terrorist group. The SAS became overnight heroes, and although the regiment is cloaked in secrecy, it has inspired more written material than any other regiment in history.

There are two methods of entry into the SAS. The first – but by no means the easiest – is through the two TA units. Selection interviews are held monthly and each candidate must first complete a 5-mile run in under 40 minutes. The selection tests last for eight alternate weekends, with a two-week camp at the end. After at least three years' service with a TA unit, troopers can apply to complete the regular 22nd SAS selection course via attachment to R Squadron. The potential recruit is then trained by both the TA and regular SAS to complete the following February or August selection. This method of entry is considered the 'back door' into the regiment, and is resented by many serving members because of the excessive help R Squadron applicants get from their TA units.

The second method follows three years' service in the regular Army and an application to SAS headquarters in Hereford. Some regiments, like the Parachute Regiment, insist that all candidates complete a pre-selection course to check their suitability to serve before recommending them for selection. The SAS selection process is split into three phases, fitness, continuation and advanced, and lasts more than two years. Troopers serve until they are no longer required, but officers can only be attached for three years.

The Army Air Corps

HISTORY The Army Air Corps was formed in 1957 from artillery observer and light liaison flights, and the first air troops were established in 1962. It was soon nicknamed the 'Teeny Weeny Airways' and was accepted as a Combat Arm in late 1973. Today helicopters have become an essential part of modern warfare, and no army could possibly win a war without them. Helicopters are used by the Infantry and the Royal Armoured Corps for reconnaissance and observation of enemy troop movements. They help gun batteries of the Royal Artillery by observing and correcting fire. Anti-tank helicopters hunt and destroy ground targets, while others carry and transport vital ammunition and stores to forward fighting units and resupply special forces behind enemy lines. There are five regiments: four are located in the UK and one in Germany.

PERSONAL CHARACTERISTICS   The corps require highly articulate soldiers and potential team leaders. Soldiers need to be physically fit, with lots of stamina, and must be prepared for a hectic life of constant exercises and movements.

WORKING CONDITIONS   In barracks work can be clean and carried out in well-ventilated hangars. Exercises can be held anywhere from training areas to commandeered roads; in the words of one officer, 'If it's flat, it's usable!'

ENTRY REQUIREMENTS   No formal qualifications needed.

POSTINGS   Anywhere in the world, but most first postings are to regiments in Germany or the UK.

The Services

HISTORY   The history of the logistic corps over the last hundred years has been one of splits and mergers, as supplies and transport were separated and then amalgamated and then separated again. The turning point came as a result of a disaster when the whole system collapsed in the Western Desert in 1942. Soon after that, all vehicle repairs were passed to the Royal Electrical and Mechanical Engineers and the old supply system was broken down and allocated to new corps. The reorganisation came to its conclusion in 1965 when the Royal Army Service Corps passed control of its remaining supply functions to the Royal Army Ordnance Corps. However, some of these functions were again merged and reorganised in late 1993. It would seem the Army is still unable to find the perfect system for supplying the modern Army.

PERSONAL CHARACTERISTICS   Soldiers need a methodical approach to paperwork in administration posts, and management skills.

WORKING CONDITIONS   Much of the soldiers' time is spent

preparing and delivering the needed supplies, any time of the day or night.

ENTRY REQUIREMENTS   No formal qualifications required.

POSTINGS   World-wide. Soldiers are usually 'trickle-posted' at two-yearly intervals, except for the Pioneers, who remain in the same posting for some time.

The Royal Logistics Corps
HISTORY   Created from the amalgamation of the Royal Army Ordnance Corps, the Catering Corps, the Royal Corps of Transport, the Royal Pioneer Corps and the Royal Engineers Postal and Courier Service. The RLC now uses computer touch-screen technology to order and move stores around.

The Royal Army Medical Corps
HISTORY   The RAMC was founded from three separate branches in 1898: the Regimental Medical System, a Medical Staff Corps of doctors, and a Hospital Corps consisting largely of nurses. The Sudan Campaign in the same year was its baptism of fire. Today the Corps has the highest-qualified professionals in the Army, and the best paid. It is headed by a Lieutenant-General, who also controls the Army dentists and the Queen Alexandra's Royal Army Nursing Corps.

The range of experience needed differs from that of their civilian counterparts, with much more emphasis on social and preventive medicine, children's doctoring, some psychology and of course pathology. The treatment of gunshot wounds is a subject few civilians will learn, but here it requires special training because, unlike most injuries, gunshot wounds cannot be stitched until all the traces of bullet and dead or infected tissue have been removed. Their motto is *In Arduis Fidelis* ('Faithful in adversity').

The Royal Electrical and Mechanical Engineers
HISTORY   The REME was formed in 1942. It has grown with the Army's mechanical sophistication and is now the largest single 'capbadge' in the Army, accounting for 10 per cent of the total strength. The REME support consists of three lines of repair: the first is the Light Aid Detachment with each mechanised and armoured regiment; the second

88

is the Armoured Workshops; and the last is the Technical Workshops in the UK, of which there are four.

The Adjutant General's Corps

HISTORY   Formed by the amalgamation of the Royal Military Police, the Royal Army Pay Corps, the Women's Royal Army Corps, the Royal Army Educational Corps, the Army Legal Corps, and all regimental clerks, the Adjutant General's Corps provides administrative support to the Army as a whole. Although it is a single corps, it in fact consists of four main branches: the Provost Branch, the Staff and Personnel Support Branch, the Educational and Training Services Branch and the Army Legal Services Branch. All the branches, except the Staff and Personnel Support Branch, retain their own capbadges. The Corps motto is *Animo Et Fide* ('With resolution and fidelity').

The Royal Army Veterinary Corps

HISTORY   The role of the Veterinary Corps declined soon after the tank replaced the horse, and in a sense the REME has replaced it. Today it finds itself caring for and supervising the training of the Army's dogs and the ceremonial horses of the Household Division. Modern training gives little time for excursions abroad, apart from postings to Sennelager in Germany.

The Royal Army Dental Corps

HISTORY   The Army recognised the need for a dental service in 1921, and a warrant was soon signed by Winston Churchill to establish one. Some 3,000 dentists served the Army during the Second World War, and the Dental Corps had 'Royal' added to its name in 1946. It became famous for having the first recorded escapee from a prisoner of war camp in 1940. In peacetime it remains a small corps with a family atmosphere. The motto is *Ex Dentibus Ensis* ('From the teeth a sword').

The Intelligence Corps

HISTORY   The 'Int' Corps was first used in the First World War. It proved unsuccessful and was phased out by the end of hostilities, only to be revived in 1940. Its main task was to interrogate prisoners, and this remains one of its prime roles. It survived beyond the war and was firmly established during the Malayan Emergency, which proved to be predominantly an intelligence war. The motto is *Manui Dat Cognitio Vires* ('Knowledge gives power to the arm').

PERSONAL CHARACTERISTICS   Soldiers need a high degree of common sense and intelligence. The ability to take responsibility is a must.

WORKING CONDITIONS   Soldiers often work in small groups or alone. Work in both Germany and the UK is in clean, modern establishments. In Northern Ireland, soldiers rarely leave their bases while in uniform. The few who work as field intelligence NCOs (undercover agent runners) are normally in their early thirties and have had at least three previous tours of the Province.

ENTRY REQUIREMENTS   A minimum of five GCSEs at Grade C or above, but preferably A Levels.

POSTINGS   World-wide. Soldiers are 'trickle-posted' and change every two years on average.

Queen Alexandra's Royal Army Nursing Corps
HISTORY   Formed in 1917 as the Women's Army Auxiliary Corps and used in a non-combatant role, its name was changed in 1918 to the Queen Mary's Army Auxiliary Corps, but it was disbanded the following year. However, due to a shortage of qualified nurses in the Army, it was reformed as the Auxiliary Territorial Service, and had a further change of name a decade later to the Women's Royal Army Nursing Corps before adopting its current name. The motto is *Suaviter in Modo, Fortiter in Re* ('Gentle in manner, resolute in deed').

CHAPTER 8

Regimental Initiation

'A good regiment is a school of manhood, honour
and selfless co-operation, and in nine cases out of
ten, a soldier is only a good soldier to the extent
that his regiment has made him so.'
Arthur Bryant, 1972

After leaving the training regiments and all their restrictions,
the young recruits embark on the journey to their chosen
regiment or corps. For some this could involve a move of a
few miles to ceremonial duties in London, while others might
find themselves on flights to Germany. But wherever they
go, they leave behind their seniority, the seniority they have
attained through months of hard work and determination.
During their time at the training regiments they will have
seen new and old recruits arrive and leave, and with each
passing off, they will have moved one step closer to the top
of the ladder.

However, on joining their regiment, they become the new
arrival again, the 'crow', 'sprog' or 'neg'. They are absorbed
into a world dominated by senior troopers, where NCOs
sit back and watch with amusement the 'character-building'
mockery that is still a part of Army life, once called the 'singlies'
subculture. This is not bullying, despite what the tabloid press
says, it is tradition, the tradition of old soldiers sending the
naive new arrival on pointless errands, often to borrow a
'long weight' from the Company Quartermaster. Admittedly,
there were cases of serious bullying in some Infantry and
Artillery regiments, especially on postings in Germany, but the
clampdown in 1988 and the massive redundancy programme
in the early 1990s has eradicated the problem.

After the new arrival has been allocated a bed-space and
bedding, one of the senior troopers or junior NCOs will be
given the responsibility of looking after him or her. The first
day is spent with a a leisurely walk around the camp and

some sightseeing. In Germany this may take the form of a visit to the nearest town or, in the case of soldiers in Hohne or Fallinbostel, a trip to the concentration camp at Belsen.

The accommodation in the UK may be in the form of six-bed rooms, with no more than a bed, wardrobe and bedside locker for furniture. In Germany many of the blocks are modern, self-contained flatlets with spartan kitchens that are hardly ever used. The washrooms are equipped with baths and showers; the open communal showers were curtained off in 1991 to reduce the possibility of homosexual encounters. Utility rooms with washing machines and tumble driers have replaced the old inadequate drying rooms. The newly decorated accommodation rooms sleep up to four and many boast fully-fitted lockers, double glazing and Flotex carpet, aptly named 'cigarette burn brown'.

Some soldiers are not so fortunate. Living in condemned blocks, with electricity provided by an improvised cable connected to another block and set up by a live-in REME technician, they sleep in cramped eight- to twelve-bed rooms. The buildings are so old that the pre-war Nazi rifle racks set in ports along crumbling painted corridors are still clearly visible.

Each soldier's bed-space is crammed with hi-fis, televisions, video recorders and computers, and each bed has its own multi-coloured duvet; those who are attempting to escape reality have cartoon characters like the Flintstones, Mickey Mouse or Postman Pat, the more vain have *Playboy* symbols. The walls are plastered with naked pin-ups, calendars, pictures of loved ones and certificates of sporting achievements and qualifications. The more 'army barmy' display SAS posters, regimental plaques and tactics and training pamphlets. Most people, however, say that no matter how hard they try, it can never really be called a home.

On the second and third days, the new arrival starts the round of interviews, starting with the Company Sergeant-Major and the Company Commander and followed by the feared Regimental Sergeant-Major. They all give the same warnings about alcohol, drugs, debt and Aids, then end with the reminder, 'And don't forget to show your face in the bar this evening . . .'

The once mandatory interview with the Commanding Officer is now rare; only a few commanding officers welcome new soldiers these days. On the other hand, new subaltern officers just out of Sandhurst are welcomed as a matter of course, which only adds to the frustration felt by many junior ranks that a two-tier Army is emerging. It is also a sign of the weakening of the family atmosphere which was cultivated by most regiments. This new attitude has almost certainly been brought about by amalgamations and the need to change, but what many commanding officers fail to realise is that the British Army's regimental system is arguably the finest structure of any of the world's fighting forces, in time of war and peace, and should be preserved.

The next port of call for soldiers posted to Germany is the local bank to open an account; most barracks are serviced by local branches of the Kreissparkasse. The branch in Hohne is typical; situated next to the Roundhouse Naafi, an old Nazi officers' mess, it has a relaxed atmosphere with helpful staff and is managed by an ex-captain from the German Army. They then go to the Pay Office to register their arrival and set up a bank credit for the payment of their monthly wages into the newly opened account. They may also be given an advance, which is paid back direct from their wages. This is no more than a token payment to give them some money for the evening.

The company bars can range in decor from the elaborate to the basic. The best are fitted with false wooden beams and large open fireplaces, with decor ranging from brass horseshoes to swords, daggers and the odd 'trophy' which is more often than not a stolen blue flashing light from a military police vehicle. The worst are no more than a set of tables, chairs and a fridge to keep the beers cold.

The regimental initiation ceremonies are mostly harmless affairs – no more than a single shot of whisky to be drunk in one go. Those regiments that took their own steps to stamp out the drunken rituals of 'regimental initiations' by allocating a senior private to act as the new arrival's 'minder', did the Army a massive favour and improved its fighting effectiveness almost overnight.

Many soldiers who experienced initiation ceremonies shrug off the experience as just harmless fun, adding that those soldiers who took it seriously were only proving that they were 'wet'. One soldier (now a sergeant), who went through the ordeal, described it as being 'the only way to be accepted'.

This need to be accepted is universal in the Army; depending on the regiment, full acceptance can take up to six months to achieve. In most armoured regiments the bonding is much quicker, mainly because working in the confines of a tank, which is often like sitting inside a wardrobe with a torch, makes friendship and tolerance essential.

The young soldiers, now with a few new friends and a hangover, spend much of the following days moving from one regimental department to another, and hardly notice the buzz of activity around them.

The soldier's working day starts at 7.30 with block jobs. Each flat member is given a job in cleaning the block or flat; these tasks are normally given out by the flat NCO. Each Monday morning the Platoon or Troop Sergeant carries out an inspection. In some regiments this is a basic-training type 'stand by your beds' inspection; in others (like many cavalry regiments, which have toned down their inspections after criticism from the ranks about invasion of privacy), it is no more than an informal walkabout, with lots of gossiping about the weekend's events. During the autumn soldiers can be seen on leaf-collecting duties, a task that still causes much complaint, given that they are supposed to be serving in a modern army.

The working days are spent killing time until Naafi break at 10, and then lunch at 12.30. During the long and often boring afternoons, NCOs disappear on 'admin' tasks, or to set up lectures and practical lessons in the field. Royal Armoured Corps and REME soldiers spend hours preparing vehicles for the next exercise, until knocking-off time at around 4.30, when they go to tea and then up to the bar.

Almost every barracks or garrison has a tank park, filled with Warriors and Challengers and soldiers working desperately inside the engine compartments. On every tank park there is sure to be an engine change, called a 'pack lift', taking place. REME technicians climb in and out of the rear compartment and shout instructions to mechanics and electricians; the expensive Rolls-Royce engine is removed and replaced in a few hours.

The new arrivals are often astounded at the mass of vehicles in these massive hangars; for the young soldier who has seen no more than five or six vehicles at any one time, this mass of over fifty tanks, armoured personnel carriers or artillery pieces is overwhelming.

Soon the new soldiers realise that they have achieved little in the Army compared to the vast amount of experience around them. Many of their comrades will have served in Northern Ireland, Bosnia and the Gulf, while many more wear the scars not of military war, but night-club war!

During the recruit's training there is instilled a sense of urgency to serve in Northern Ireland, because the Province is considered 'the ultimate test of soldiering'. This desire to be tested is often short-lived upon arrival in the Province, but many still listen with relish as the 'old soldiers' describe in great detail their personal accounts of urban war, including the riots and sniper fire in the Republican areas of Belfast; many with extra colour and exaggeration to add to the effect and to boost their own uninteresting deeds.

Some soldiers find themselves posted directly to Northern Ireland after completion of training. In the case of some support corps they are attached to a regiment for up to two years. These soldiers, including many women from the Intelligence Corps, are almost immediately thrown in at the deep end, where the need to grow up fast can be paramount to survival.

Those in many of the non-infantry regiments complain that there is little to excite them except the annual tour to Canada. The seemingly endless exercises on Salisbury Plain or live-firing training do little to encourage soldiers to stay on. Regiments on ceremonial duty are even worse affected. With the constant inspections and rotation of guard duties, there is little to stir the imagination, except the collection of phone numbers from female admirers.

Regiments have been warned of the need to keep their men busy, and most have taken steps to improve the 'boredom at work' syndrome by organising adventure training exercises in most parts of the world. Sadly, the reduction in adventure training lodges in Bavaria has not helped this problem. Regiments now have to go to great expense to send soldiers skiing or rock climbing at lodges that they once owned, with entrepreneurs leaving the forces and setting up lodges of their own to fill the need for inexpensive adventure training. Ultimately the ones to lose out are the soldiers.

Exercises

The young soldier's first taste of realistic soldiering is in the form of combat-training exercises. Whether on Salisbury Plain or the Hohne ranges, the regiments form battle groups, comprised of both Infantry and Armoured units with the support of other combat arms from every part of the Army. In high-intensity operations the battle group is the major front-line unit involved in the fighting. All combat regiments work within a battle group or brigade, and much of the additional training soldiers receive is tested in the field in these formations.

Regimental commanding officers are informed of exercises months in advance, and the slow trickle of information from the regiment's headquarters creates a burst of activity on vehicle parks as new and old soldiers prepare. Once the regiment has prepared the vehicles for the exercise it moves from its camp to the training area.

At this stage, the battle group has not yet formed, but is still in its regiments for special-to-arms training. In the infantry, debussing and clearing enemy position exercises are practised to remove the cobwebs, followed by training with the Armoured squadrons to practise combined frontal and counter-attacks. The Artillery's forward observation officers complete in-depth training, both in the rapid deployment and on their speed of delivery of fire missions. The Army Air Corps' Gazelle and Lynx helicopters not only provide the battle group commander with an additional rapid strike capability, but can also give units the opportunity to conduct reconnaissance flights, to check the terrain and seek out 'killing zones'. They also transport ground troops around the battlefield.

Once the special-to-arms training has been completed, battle groups form up together to commence realistic battlefield exercises. The battle group headquarters is a highly sophisticated operational command centre and is the brain behind the force. From the Sultan command vehicles, officers and experienced soldiers control everything from Intelligence reports to troop movements. Using the latest secure communications, they receive and transmit all information on the enemy's dispositions, weather reports (vital for air support), logistical requirements and future battle objectives. In war this command centre would be a priority target for enemy special forces, so protection is vital, and it is provided by a section of supporting infantry as well as Artillery Rapier air defence systems. On peacetime exercises, however, these units are rarely deployed.

It is rare for a new soldier to be posted directly into the battle group command centre, as the responsibility of the job requires the most experienced soldiers in the regiment. Pathfinder or reconnaissance troops provide the battle group with a forward screening force and are considered the elite of the battalion or regiment. Soldiers have to complete at least three years' regimental service before consideration is given to their secondment, and because of the nature of their work and training received, many of them go on to attempt the SAS selection course.

On today's modern battlefield the delivery of a quick but powerful punch falls to the sabre squadrons of the Cavalry and the Infantry. Equipped with the advanced Challenger tank and Warrior armoured personnel carrier, they are of paramount importance to the battle group's success, because no matter how sophisticated an army is, it will always need ground troops to clear and occupy in-depth positions.

The battle group's commander also has the capability to call down a devastating artillery barrage, which greatly enhances the chance of success in defeating an enemy. The young gunners of the Artillery can expect to spend a few years in a battery before being considered for attachment to a forward observation crew. These small closely-knit teams, commanded by an experienced officer, instruct the batteries to provide fire missions via the Army's latest target-acquisition equipment. The forward observation officers (FOOs) can instruct the battery at the press of a button to fire a salvo on to a predetermined target. This speed and effi-ciency allows front-line troops to call down a fire mission in minutes, in support of either attacking or defensive operations.

A major combat element of the battle group is the combat engineers. Their job is to prepare a route for the unit's advance or withdrawal. This may mean bull-dozing breaches, blasting a way through minefields with Giant Vipers, flailing the ground with Aardvark armoured vehicles or destroying any other obstacle with the 165 mm on their armoured vehicle. The Royal Engineers' small units give the young soldier a great deal of responsibility very quickly.

The Army has always prided itself on its ability to bring units together for mixed training exercises world-wide. This has increased over the last five years because many units need additional training to prepare them for the many new operational commitments and the emerging global peace-keeping operations.

One problem the Army faces over exercises and training is the reduction in good training areas, including the handing back of the Soltau–Luneberg training area in Germany. Although the MoD has said it is seeking alternatives, no new areas have become available yet. Given time, new exercise facilities will be provided but until then, the battle groups will have to hone their skills in camp or on the few remaining live-firing ranges in Europe.

The new soldiers' first exercise will be a mixture of excitement, tiredness, and boredom, with the odd egg 'banjo' (sandwich) and many 'shovel recces' (toilet trips)! They can find themselves catapulted into a three-week field exercise where the days start before dawn and end after dusk. Sleep is taken at any opportunity, and many tank gunners do little else. For the engineers or support elements it can be days of restless boredom followed by hours of frantic activity. In Germany and some parts of Salisbury Plain restrictions on movement at night can halt an advance or attack dead in its tracks, a problem that adds to the frustration but does give soldiers a chance to rest.

The nights are broken down into two-hour sentry duties in cold, wet trenches, or radio 'stags' in dry but finger-numbing, freezing turrets with the constant hiss of radio 'mush' adding to the discomfort. Those not on guard duty sleep restlessly in their 'maggots' on the hot oily engine decks, covered by a green plastic sheet which is intended to hold in the heat and keep out the wet, but does neither.

The tradition of ending an exercise with a 'smoker' or big bonfire, has been totally abolished by the Army. Once considered a great morale booster that brought soldiers together and allowed them to burn off any excess energy before returning to camp, it is now regarded as an unacceptable ritual.

The Role of Women

The use of women in war has always been a complex issue, often causing vehement arguments and disagreements within the ranks of the armed services. Women would relish the opportunity to take on combat roles, happy that they could do the job just as well as, or even better than, their male counterparts.

The 'invisibility' of women and the unshakeable prejudice against their use in combat is slowly crumbling away, but more so outside the British Army than in it. The United States and Israeli armies, two highly respected fighting forces, both employ women in front-line combat roles. Israel has even gone so far as to have female instructors at its Armoured Training Depot, believing, correctly, that males listen and absorb more information if it is given by a female instructor. Clearly the position of women will improve as the Army faces falling recruitment figures and increasing resignations, but the road to combat is still likely to be a long one.

Tomorrow's front line will surely include women; nothing can stop the evolution. However, it is unlikely to come about until some nagging questions have been answered once and for all. Have women got the capacity to be aggressive? Can they fire weapons of mass destruction? How will their presence, or more importantly, their death in combat, affect other soldiers? Ironically, these questions cannot be answered until women have first served in the front line.

The Army argues that there are practical considerations against the use of women as fighting soldiers. Canada had been employing women as combat soldiers for many years, but they found that they do not make the best foot soldiers. Infantry troops are expected to be able to carry a burgen, a weapon, spare small arms ammunition, extra food and at least two mortar or anti-tank munitions, a total weight of more than 120 lbs, across arduous terrain for 30 or more miles. Many women who attempted Canadian infantry training, failed. Some claimed that this was because the infantry instructors were too harsh, but one instructor retorted, 'Women recruits who volunteer for infantry training do so knowing they will work alongside males. Whatever the man is expected to do, she must do also. We do not lower our standards for anyone. If she fails she fails, and if she passes, she passes just like the men.' In some regiments such as the Artillery, Armour and Engineers, of course, these physical problems do not arise and women can achieve the stringent requirements.

This is in fact a generational issue. Tradition, supported by media pressure, has created a stereotypical attitude towards women in the forces, and it does not help having some senior officers opposed to women in the Army. Yet attitudes are changing, with women taking up positions that were once male dominated, and whereas once the suggestion of a woman driving a tank or building a bridge was met with mocking laughter, now it is greeted with 'Why not?' The Gulf War undoubtedly helped in changing opinions but not to the extent that some commentators claim. Admittedly, women that once were only chauffeurs to brigadiers were seconded into driving vital supplies to forward troops during the war, often coming within sight of the front line. However, this was not due to a sudden change of heart regarding sexual equality by commanders but more a necessity owing to the excessive manpower shortages. Military commanders saw the use of women, many of whom were without a role to play, as necessary to maintain the momentum of the attack. American military commanders deployed women to front-line positions as a matter of course, and in particularly to operate the Patriot missile defence systems in Israel. Other countries have also opened the door for women in combat regiments.

But not every woman joins in to be actively involved in fighting. In fact, in a recent survey, only 1 per cent of women said that if given the choice they would take up a position in a front line combat regiment as a fighting soldier. Senior commanders also emphasise the practicalities to support their view – 'A man and a woman cannot share the same trench or sleep in close proximity on the back decks of a tank.'

One argument in favour of the Army's view is the fact that troop and civilian morale would be severely dented if female soldiers deployed to front-line regiments were killed in action. Civilians shrug this off, saying that it is their job. But this attitude would surely change if our televisions showed pictures of male soldiers offloading bodybag after bodybag containing servicewomen killed in a war. Jingoism usually wanes after such sights, but it is a sight we are sure to see in the future, perhaps not in the British Army in the immediate future but certainly in an army that allows women into the front line.

In civilian occupations changes have already occurred. Not only do women now carry firearms as police officers or political bodyguards but also on undercover operations in Northern Ireland, alongside such elites as the SAS and MI5. With the millennium zooming towards us, it is surely time for outdated sentiment and tradition to be put to one side in the interests of national defence, and for women to be allowed to enter combat regiments if – and it is a big if – they can complete the physical training without standards being lowered. Unless the Army is prepared to do this, few young women will choose a career in the military. In the words of one civilian girl who enquired about joining the Army but took it no further: 'I saw the Army as a good career choice with the possibility of travel, excitement, variety, advancement and the chance to be a "hero", just like those who returned from the Gulf. The opportunity to be proud of my job and stand out from the rest of the crowd at the same time compelled me to find out more. But the jobs available to women were limited to administrative roles or playing second fiddle to the men. I think I'm worth more than that.' Yet she was considered by the Recruiting Sergeant to be a perfect recruit with two A Levels and seven GCSEs.

With the fading of old values and with operations requiring soldiers to hold the delicate position of peace-keepers between warring factions such as in Bosnia or Rwanda, the particular skills women possess can be of great value. The need for soldiers in front-line regiments to have the skills for these delicate situations will become even more apparent in the future. They are skills that women possess naturally, and their employment with these regiments, and not just as clerks or technicians, could help to defuse potentially hostile situations.

Racism

The armed forces are an equal opportunity employer bound by the provisions of the Race Relations Act to recruit from all ethnic groups, yet the Army has been dogged by revelations in the press of widespread racism. No officer can deny that there are cases of racial harassment in certain regiments, and the revelations certainly came as no surprise to the many black and Asian soldiers, but to say it is a 'widespread' problem is somewhat misleading. Even so, the Army takes the accusations very seriously. In the words of one major, 'Racism is no longer an issue, it's a serious problem.'

This was highlighted in a 1992–3 recruiting survey that concluded that only 1.3 per cent of applicants, and only 0.8 per cent of entrants, were non-white. The Army had, until then, always thought that there was a good representation of all ethnic groups within its ranks, and that its personnel represented every community in Britain. However, it was certainly untrue then and is probably untrue now. The Army has always, quite simply, struggled to accept blacks.

It has tried hard to stamp out the problem and to increase its appeal to different ethnic groups by supplying specialist clothing and equipment for recruits bound by their religious beliefs. For example, Sikhs are required by their religion to wear turbans, and the wearing of the normal military head-dress was not allowed. The Army turned to the Sikh community for an answer. The solution was simple and cost-effective; turbans in the same colour as the normal head-dress could be worn, with the regiment's capbadge placed in the centre. However, few Sikhs took to the idea because they were ridiculed by other soldiers because some – and it must be said they are a minority – despise others who are different.

The Director of Army Recruiting is involved in a new survey on ethnic enlistment. But although this was due to be completed in May 1995, by the end of 1994 only 52 per cent of the questionnaires sent to Army personnel had been returned, as opposed to 65 per cent from the RAF. This survey will, in any case, do little to change the balance in ethnic recruiting, although it will help monitor the initiatives put in place by the MoD and could help, in the long term, to identify possible areas of success and failure.

The Army has also moved to offer personnel, regardless of creed or colour, the opportunity of any employment during their service, and to its credit it has established a new branch to cover equal opportunities. The new branch, under a full colonel, is based on the Director of Women (Army); it comes under the Director of Manning (Army) and is known as M4. It covers a wide variety of issues but its main task will be the introduction of equal opportunities training. Although senior commanders have always tried to be fair and allow soldiers to progress purely on their abilities and not their colour, they have often failed.

Army recruiters have attended ethnic sensitivity training sessions under consultants to publicly run companies like Equality Associates. Recruiters at all levels have also been involved in initiatives with Asian and other ethnic groups at community centres and youth organisations, helping to promote the Army and dispel the old image of racism and arrogance, which was always wrong and totally unjustified. The Army has its faults but when they are highlighted it does try to rectify them immediately.

Bullying

An investigation into allegations of bullying that was begun in 1988 found that most proven cases were carried out at basic training depots. In light of this, new initiatives were introduced to eradicate it. Today, the problem has all but gone, even within that most aggressive of regiments, the Parachute Regiment. Today, young soldiers are quicker to report incidents than they once were, alerting officers who can stop the problem immediately. Previously, young soldiers were afraid to speak out, which only dragged the problem underground and caused it to proliferate. Victims were often driven to attempt suicide or to try to kill the offenders during live-firing exercises. Senior NCOs are now more compassionate, mainly because they were often themselves victims of bullying a decade ago, and this brutality is a thing of the past. Today, soldiers still get drunk but they do not go looking for a one-sided fight with their own.

Alcohol, Drugs and the Standards and Discipline Paper

Alcohol remains a problem, and has become the highest contributory factor in violent crime in the Army. In early 1994 the Adjutant General, General Sir Michael Wilkes, realising that there was a growing discipline problem within Field Army regiments, issued a new code of conduct entitled the 'Standards and Discipline Paper'. It was sent direct to every commanding officer in the Army, including every Territorial Army unit. The paper was not just directed at senior officers or those in the chain of command, but at everyone in positions of responsibility. It said that the Army expected high standards of the younger soldiers and that all ranks should seek a high regard for a 'sense of duty, loyalty, self-discipline, self-sacrifice and respect'.

It also expressed concern about alcohol abuse saying, 'It is of concern that the average consumption of alcohol by service personnel remains very high and is a major cause of impaired efficiency, disciplinary problems and accidents.'

Because of media claims of widespread drug use, which were almost certainly exaggerated, the paper also included advice on this problem. No one can deny that there is some illegal use of controlled drugs, but it is normally restricted to small 'closed' groups of very naive young soldiers. Gaining access to such groups, whether as a potential user or as an investigator, is almost impossible. These small groups in fact total only 1 per cent of Army personnel but it is 1 per cent too many. The initiative to test all ranks randomly and without warning, copied from the US Army, has certainly helped reduce the problem, especially experiments by the curious. The Adjutant General's paper stressed that the use of illegal substances 'may lead to dismissal, or in the case of an officer, to resign his commission even if military charges are not brought'.

With regard to bullying, initiation ceremonies (another problem nearly eradicated) and racial discrimination it said, 'The responsibility for the well being of subordinates rests with commanders at all times. Abuse or disregard of that responsibility amounts to neglect. Initiation ceremonies involving assault, humiliation, intimidation, racial discrimination and the abuse of alcohol are not to be tolerated.'

On the subject of sex, it said, 'Sexual harassment is unacceptable and homosexuality is incompatible with military service.' The Adjutant General also identified potential problems with sexual relationships between officers and non-commissioned ranks, saying that it would 'undermine a well-ordered structure and cannot be tolerated'. It added, 'While marriage between officers and other ranks is not prohibited, it causes difficulties and should be discouraged.'

While the paper was warmly accepted because it suggested much-needed remedies to some ongoing problems, it is hardly likely to reduce the consumption of alcohol, especially on operational tours overseas, where beer is the only release from weeks of tension. The quick pint down at the local will always be a part of the soldier's culture; nothing will ever change that. But the cases of alcohol abuse in the Army are certainly a cause for concern. That is not to say the Army is manned by a bunch of drunken squaddies. Again the problem is with a minority, just like civilian hooliganism. As with bullying and racism, a small group is focusing the British media's interest on the Army as a whole and this affects both civilian and military morale. I believe the Army is still the best there is, despite some bad press. Its soldiers are volunteers who have chosen to protect this country and its people from aggressors anywhere in the world. All too often the papers do not give credit to those soldiers, for example, who raise thousands of pounds for charity, or to those commanders who are using the Army's budget to enhance facilities, accommodation and eradicate the problems of the past.

CHAPTER 9

A Soldier's Life

'There's no doubt that German girls are bending
over backwards to please British soldiers!'
Kate Aitken, 1959

The British Army provides men and women with the opportunity to explore and experience a part of life that no civilian
occupation can offer. Soldiers could find themselves posted
to any part of the world, including the United Kingdom,
Germany, the Falkland Islands, Brunei, Cyprus, Gibraltar,
Belize or Hong Kong, with the opportunity to take part in
exercises in Australasia, North America, the Middle East and
several African countries. They can expect to live and work in
many diverse environments, from desert and the jungle to the
Arctic. Today's modern Army is putting much emphasis on
the development of character and leadership at every level.
Soldiers now mature more quickly and acquire a sense of
responsibility from a very early age. The Army has always
been an elite institution, with all its ranks locked together
in a kind of united, unforgettable family. It is an institution
that many of its ranks have died to preserve.

Within this family the soldiers live, sleep and fight together.
They learn each other's strengths and weaknesses, and when
an individual leaves it is like losing a brother or sister. That is
why it is sometimes difficult for new soldiers to be accepted.
The outsider has to earn the group's respect, and within some
small Corps, acceptance is only achieved with hard work and
in isolation. Once accepted, however, they become a part of
a 'closed' team of soldiers, and it is this inherent culture that
forms the foundation of a soldier's life.

To be an individual within this group means alienation and
harassment. The 'loner' who pursues hobbies or studies for
qualifications is often met with scorn and teasing, although
it is normally these very people who are promoted most
quickly. Because of this too few soldiers take advantage

of the wide range of opportunities available within the Army, although time restrictions and the lack of information available from some regiments compounds the problem. With units still seriously under-staffed, it is not surprising that they refuse to allow soldiers the time away from normal garrison duties. However, it is ultimately the soldier's responsibility to keep trying.

Weekends

In Britain the mass exodus of soldiers on Friday afternoons leaves many camps deserted; those who remain do so because they are on guard duty, or quite simply because of a lack of cash.

In Germany most soldiers become creatures of habit; with the shops closing early on Saturday and closed all day on Sunday, the weekends are spent glued to the television or watching videos, with as many as eight videos being swapped between rooms. The introduction of the British Broadcasting Service, a mix of both BBC and Independent television and radio programmes, in the late 1970s, was a well-needed boost to morale but few improvements have been made over the last decade and the programmes cater more for a family audience than garrison soldiers. Those with little interest in television spend hours playing 'Sonic the Hedgehog' or some other compulsive computer game.

During the summer, football competitions are organised by NCOs, and these always bring out a mass of soldiers to participate or shout encouragement. Those with cars go to local swimming baths in search of fun and female frolics, while the more adventurous visit Denmark, Bavaria or Eastern Europe, sleeping on the floors of multi-storey car parks and absorbing the sights, sounds and local customs.

Sergeants often sympathise with the boring plight of soldiers at weekends. Their offers of Sunday lunch are often taken up eagerly, and many 'singlies' stay all weekend, often weeding the garden or baby-sitting.

Alcohol

As we have already seen, drinking plays an important part in Army life, with all ranks, from private to officer, provided with the facilities to drink the nights away in the officers', sergeants' or corporals' messes, the Naafi bar, or the company or squadron bars. By midnight, single soldiers disappear to town to local 'squaddie' discos, often after the consumption of surprisingly large amounts of beer. Some soldiers take consumption to extremes by drinking themselves into oblivion, with no apparent pleasure, either to show their prowess or because of immaturity.

At the disco, they endeavour to acquire a partner for the remainder of the evening. There is always a supply of women at 'squaddie' drinking holes, and many are prepared to accept the drunken soldiers with open arms. One girl even went to the extent of locking a young gunner in her home for four days. The military police were finally called in by the unit and the embarrassed soldier was freed, swearing to live the remainder of his life in celibacy.

There is a lot of inter-regimental rivalry, and the consumption of large quantities of alcohol breeds a need in the soldiers to prove that their regiment is the best, particularly among the Infantry and Royal Horse Artillery, who regard themselves as the elite. The fights that result are usually spontaneous and end quickly, with the offenders being parted to cool down or in some cases to be arrested by the Military Police. Most fights are started in night-clubs and are usually over girls. Another cause is stolen beer, known by soldiers as 'mine-sweeping'.

Crimes of violence resulting in common assault and actual bodily harm are nearly always committed after heavy drinking sessions and over 60 per cent of all courts martial in the Army are drink-related. There are limits to the punishments commanding officers can inflict within the regiment, and these can range from fines or restriction of privileges to 28 days in jail or demotion one rank in the case of an NCO. Anything that may require a more severe punishment is sent for trial by court martial. Soldiers have the right to elect for court martial if they refuse to accept the commanding officer's punishment, which very rarely happens. If it does, the soldier is usually marched outside by the Regimental Sergeant-Major and told in no uncertain terms to accept the punishment or be prepared for every available guard duty until the date of the court martial. In the Army it is hard to buck the system or beat authority at its own game.

Violence in the Army needs to be compared with that in

an average inner-city area. Taking into account the violent and often aggressive nature of soldiering today, the cases of fighting are on a par with, or even lower than, in the civilian world. No matter how advanced the Army becomes, soldiers will always be prone to bouts of mindless violence.

Many young soldiers who have girlfriends or boyfriends when they join the Army find it very difficult to continue normal relationships, especially when posted overseas. Many love affairs fade or collapse, with the defiant soldier pinning the rejection letter to the platoon's notice boards so that everyone can have a laugh. Even relationships that involve service personnel, as between a male soldier and a female soldier or the daughter of a senior NCO, are almost impossible to keep going, particularly with the macho ethos of barrack-room life, where men are more prone to bragging than loyalty to their girlfriends. Soldiers will often share sexual secrets with their comrades and pass around revealing photographs of their supposed loved ones, which only adds to the joke. Even soldiers who do not get involved find that the barrack-room 'mob' will give the girl the impression that he has given away secrets, which nearly always ends with doubt being instilled in her mind and can end relationships. In the UK there is no such problem because many soldiers can catch a lift home at weekends, and so the opportunity to have girlfriends or boyfriends away from barracks and from the 'rumour machine' greatly increases the chances of the relationship lasting.

Many single soldiers leaving the Army give as their reason the excessive last-minute notification of guard duties or excessive work for 'Keeping the Army in the Public Eye' events. These duties naturally create doubt, uncertainty and insecurity in sweethearts who become impatient with the soldier's apparent unreliability, and promising relationships can be destroyed overnight.

Despite these drawbacks, many officers are surprised at the ease with which soldiers can find partners. and particularly abroad, with the obvious language difference. Even the most introverted soldier is now showing up at company parties with a partner.

Debt

A major problem facing new recruits to many regiments is debt. Although soldiers stationed in this country are financially worse off than those abroad, with no additions to pay such as the Local Overseas Allowance, the debt problem here is much less acute than in Germany. This is because British banks are much more careful when authorising loans and giving credit. Young soldiers arriving at their regiments in Germany are likely to be no more than 18 years old. They may never have been abroad before, and soon after moving in with their new flatmates they will feel the need to emulate them. Their bed-spaces are filled with an array of electrical gadgets and within a short time the new soldiers will obtain the common charge card and budget account from the Naafi, and be well on the way to ordering their own gadgets. Few will bother to work out the interest being charged, which can amount to more than 25 per cent, while the interest on a German bank loan is less than 15 per cent.

Young soldiers can therefore quickly find themselves deep in debt, with little money from their wages to live on. For many the problem does not stop there; some feel the need to go one better and buy a car from a soldier who is also in debt but has realised the problem. The eager soldiers find the bank more than accommodating and within a few days an excessive loan has been granted, the soldier buys the car and drinks away the remainder. German banks are more than happy to provide such loans, knowing that the Army will act as guarantor and ultimately as its debt collector.

Some soldiers have hire-purchase agreements that go well beyond their means. Most end up turning to the Pay Office for help. This can result in a severe reprimand, with the Paymaster taking over the soldier's wages and agreeing with the creditors to pay off each debt monthly at a reduced rate. Others simply fall behind with their payments and throw final demands in the bin, often in the hope that the problem will just disappear. This never happens, of course, and the problem only becomes apparent when the creditor bounces a cheque. Allowing a cheque to bounce is against military law, and the soldier will be charged. A minority of soldiers revert to selling the goods they have bought at knock-down prices.

To combat these problems, most regiments now have a

system that requires all debts and loans to be registered, but many rely on the individual to come forward and register their new purchases. In the case of bank loans, however, the Paymaster must sign the loan form, which does help to keep higher debts under control.

Many single soldiers are normally broke by the middle of the month, with many having spent their wages paying back loans from room-mates. Sergeant-majors can only sit back and watch with resignation as the young soldiers happily blow their entire month's wages in one night, with no consideration for the remainder of the month.

Marriage

Debt among married men is much lower than among single soldiers even though they are subject to the 'Schrank Syndrome', when newly married couples purchase large German wall units to replace the army-issue furniture.

Some soldiers get married simply to attain privacy, while others will marry on leave, virtually on the spur of the moment, often because of a fear of losing the sweetheart from back home. Recruits who are already married are looked on more favourably, if only because there is less chance of divorce later, and therefore less regimental involvement.

Over the last five years the Army has improved conditions for many wives and the attitude of senior officers towards their welfare has altered. 'Soldiers vote with their feet,' is how one colonel put it, and added, 'Married soldiers usually leave because of their wives' discontent, and to keep their families together.'

There has also been a marked improvement in the attitudes of many senior NCOs' and officers' wives, who once believed they held the same rank and status as their husbands – something that always caused hostility and resentment among junior ranks and their wives, particularly new arrivals. But over the last five years many of the older rankers and officers have taken redundancy and left the Army, opening the way for younger soldiers to move up and ease the problem; although it has not totally disappeared, it is far better now.

Many soldiers prefer to marry their sweethearts from home, mainly because they have not been out with other soldiers and so have no 'reputation'. Unfortunately, many have found out to their cost that this can also be a major disadvantage, as they have no accurate idea of Army life. A young 17- or 18-year-old bride may be filled with excitement at the prospect of breaking away from her boring civilian life and family home to live abroad and have her own flat and independence; most view their move as one long holiday.

The bride's arrival, penniless, in a strange place and an empty flat, miles from home and with no friends, is often demoralising; many become homesick and return home within a year; their marriage is then on the slippery slope to divorce. Other couples go through a phase of arguments, mainly about money. Soldiers have always been prone to exaggeration on leave, not least where money is concerned. The new bride quickly realises that her expectations of a good life will not be fulfilled, and the talk of good wages, cheap nights out and a car are all dreams.

The welfare of Army wives in Britain has become of increasing concern to many regimental families' officers; these experienced rankers try hard to lessen the culture shock of military life. Many younger married junior ranks are still finding themselves isolated, however, with many senior ranks buying their own homes and moving away from married quarters on the 'patch', taking with them the help and advice that many young marriages need to survive. There can also be divisions between successful couples, who find themselves rising within a select social circle, and those who are not so successful, who become increasingly more isolated. The problem can often be made worse by the regimental hierarchy.

Language can also play its part in isolating the new young wife from the outside world, particularly in Germany. Many new brides will not have mastered even the most basic of German phrases, so their access to the better-priced shopping malls is reduced and they are restricted to weekly shopping sprees from service establishments, or to catalogues.

For the young recruit joining a regiment abroad after trade training, settling in can be made more difficult with a teenage bride in tow, and many are unable to cope emotionally. Their wives fare worse, with no marriage skills, and they feel totally helpless and out of their depth. Sometimes the young wife may have been told not to talk to other 'snooping' wives, particularly officers' wives because they will 'only report back to the CO', so she will close the door and shut herself off from the outside world.

The Army has tried to reduce such stresses with the introduction of wives' clubs, normally run by the Commanding Officer's wife. These clubs meet regularly and members visit new wives to the regiment and try to make them feel at home. Other professional organisations, like the Soldiers', Sailors' and Airmen's Families Association (SSAFA), call on new arrivals and check that they are all right, but getting the balance right between intrusion and necessary intervention whilst respecting privacy is always difficult.

The problem with SSAFA is its close links with the chain of command, thus confidentiality cannot be guaranteed. This problem brought about Home-Start, a semi-official organisation run by specially trained Army wives to befriend and advise young brides. They offer complete confidentiality. It has worked well and has now gained official funding. Another initiative that is also Army funded and has worked very well, not just for married men and their wives but also for single soldiers, is HIVEs (Help Information Volunteer Exchanges), which combine advice bureaux, coffee shops and clearing houses for new voluntary activities. They also provide service personnel with a more human face in giving advice and help. Over the last five years the number of both Home-Starts and HIVEs has trebled, and now one or both can be found in nearly every garrison in the Army.

Promotion

Any ambitious soldier feels a need for promotion, not just for the financial rewards, but also to gain responsibility and move up the social and leadership ladder. There is no given time-scale in most regiments for promotion to Lance-Corporal. In some infantry regiments it can happen as quickly as six months, while in others it can take as long as six years!

Promotion to the Corporals' Mess brings with it a new social circle, but also increased financial commitments, like mess-dress and bar bills; there is also the regular contribution to the Summer and Christmas Balls and, depending on how adventurous the mess committee is, there may also be the monthly fancy-dress parties.

For most new lance corporals, however, there is a more

pressing need than parties; this is the need to have a say in the regiment they serve. Each month there is a Corporals' Mess meeting, which brings all the NCOs together in a quasi-democratic forum; they discuss and vote on relevant issues, from subscription charges to charity donations, but in the end it is always the Regimental Sergeant-Major who has the ultimate say.

Promotion brings with it many perks: a single room, no block jobs, extra pay, respect and social status. Promotion also requires many soldiers to change their behaviour and act according to the accepted norm, something they may find difficult. Many regimental officers find it difficult to identify future sergeant-majors, because even the most promising young NCOs can wake up one day and decide that they have had enough or resign because they feel they have been left behind.

The promotion ladder is held firmly in place by regimental commanding officers and the Manning and Records Office. Who climbs the ladder is decided at the annual promotions conference at the regimental headquarters, at which all company, squadron or battery commanders put names forward to the Adjutant and Commanding Officer. The Regimental Sergeant-Major, whose power of veto is stronger than any other in the room, is consulted. A shake of his head can end a soldier's promotion chances for another year. One young regimental sergeant-major said, 'Lance-Corporal is the hardest rank to acquire, and the easiest to lose.'

There is also the junior NCOs' cadre, which in many regiments is completed yearly or biannually. This is a course consisting of field training, map-reading, and for the infantry, platoon and section attacks. Most applicants are also sent on adventure training exercises to build their leadership skills, and soon after passing off, the promotions are published on regimental orders.

How the new NCOs are treated within the platoon will depend upon their attitude. The need for good judgement and tact will be important, as will their ability to establish the right basis of give and take; they must ensure that the soldiers do their job, however unpopular that might make them. Some new lance-corporals try not to be too officious, but there is a fine line between being 'pushy' and being 'a push-over'.

Promotion to Corporal is more significant and more formalised, because it usually involves moving into a command position, whether of a section or a tank. The commanders' training course will be completed; from lance-corporal upwards, courses will decide future promotions. Infantry regiments send their aspiring corporals on a twelve-week Section Commanders' course. The first six weeks are spent in Brecon, which requires a high degree of fitness. The last six weeks are run by the Small Arms School Corps and complete the weapons and range qualification course. Armoured Corps corporals complete the Tank Commanders' course at Bovington, and most other arms and corps have their own equivalents.

The position of Corporal, or 'full screw' in Army slang, is halfway to senior NCO, but applicants for further advancement must first pass the Certificate of Promotion to gain the rank of Sergeant; this includes communication skills and military calculations. With the well-publicised redundancy programme removing a large portion of experienced sergeants, the Army has been forced to fill the gap with younger corporals. This has created a vacuum, leaving junior ranks depleted. This is a problem that is unlikely to be rectified in the near future, especially with so many soldiers leaving the Army in their first five years. However, this can only be good news for other ambitious recruits!

CHAPTER 10

The Future

'Gorbachev changed a generation, and the young should never forget it.'

Boris Yeltsin, 1991

Historically the Army has always resisted change, whether in the 1920s, the 1960s or the 1990s. It opposed and resented the 'Options for Change' proposals, until, that is, the difficulties experienced during the Gulf War, when manpower shortages – that had been consistently denied by many regiments – suddenly came to a head. Those regiments that were ordered to prepare for war soon found themselves requesting additional soldiers. Senior Army commanders realised that change was needed when by the time the ground offensive started every regiment in the Army was represented in some way. One infantry regiment went to the extreme with 27 different capbadges within its ranks. In the course of only a few years it has retreated in orderly fashion, regrouping and defending its new positions with dogged determination. The most remarkable thing about the Army is not that it has changed so much, but that it has changed so little, even with the large-scale amalgamations and disbandments. Today's soldiers are better trained, better clothed and better fed than ever before. Relationships between officers and other ranks are now much easier.

The current shape of the Army has been moulded by a series of compromises, and although some soldiers from merged regiments would argue that there has been a sell-out, this is almost certainly untrue. Soldiers have always been exceedingly loyal to their 'regimental family'.

But for all the modifications that have been introduced, the Army has largely come out on top, although it has been unable to keep the old regimental system in place in some new regiments, especially those in the Infantry and Royal

Armoured Corps, which have seen many of their old and new amalgamations swallowed up.

Some young officers believe the old regimental system had overstayed its welcome anyway, complaining that it was wasteful in terms of administration and training costs. On the other hand, the regimental system or 'family' gives soldiers a sense of belonging.

It works well to fortify soldiers under constant strain, as in Northern Ireland and Bosnia, and there is no good reason why it should be changed.

Apart from the Infantry and Armoured Corps, the rest of the Army has managed to weather the change, albeit in different forms, and some units, like the Royal Artillery, have actually expanded and strengthened rather than dissolved and weakened in recent years.

The restructuring programme will go on into the next century. The Army now finds itself overcommitted, and Britain's commitments are likely to increase rather than diminish over the next five years. The result will be a need for more soldiers rather than better equipment, something that is only now becoming apparent to our political masters.

Over the next few years political talks and negotiations in Northern Ireland may lead to a compromise on a united Ireland. With the help of American money the burden for the Republic of Ireland government will be greatly reduced. Peace will allow Britain to reduce considerably the current troops stationed in the province from 18 regiments to six, three from the home-based Royal Irish Regiment and three British regiments (which are sure to be withdrawn in the long term).

This will give the Government the opportunity to deploy British regiments as part of United Nations peace-keeping forces in troubled countries in Africa and elsewhere, a desire that was first expressed during the Nato summit in late 1994. Angola and Zaire have both suffered recent internal conflicts, and Liberia, Somalia and the Sudan continue to be immersed in civil wars that have starved its people for years. The sending of troops to Rwanda was a move towards achieving this goal, and served as a dress rehearsal for military commanders to fine tune their tactics.

Some sceptics argue that the Army will be moving away from

one trouble spot to another, destined to become entangled in complicated civil wars, as the Americans were in Somalia. Others believe that Britain needs to be seen as a leader in world peace, if necessary overtaking the United States in brokering its own peace negotiations. The only question over these UN duties is whether the armed forces, in particular the Army, are large enough to cope with the extra burdens.

The Army's Structure

Many military commanders believe that the future for Britain's defence does not rest solely in the hands of the Germany-based Mobile Reaction Force, although that certainly plays an important part. The transition of the Army Air Corps into two air cavalry brigades is the next logical step towards a rapid (non-nuclear) strike capability. Britain also needs to improve its rapid deployment capability and the new air brigades would certainly help do that. During the Iraqi troops concentration of forces on the Kuwait border in October 1994, the MoD had no rapid deployment capability and sent a contingent of Royal Marines instead. At the same time the 1st Armoured Division in Germany was put on stand-by. However, this armoured division would have needed three to six weeks to deploy to the region. On the other side of the Atlantic, the American Airborne Divisions were deployed within 24 hours and a major part of that force was the 6th Cavalry with its three squadrons of Longbow Apache Attack Helicopters. This rapid deployment of troops was also helped by the mass of armour the Americans had left in the region. Europe, however, can no longer expect the United States to be the 'lone crusader' in enforcing world peace.

Although the helicopter-based airmobile brigades are not due for formation until the end of the century, the recruits joining the ranks of the Army Air Corps now are its future pilots and navigators, and the Air Corps has already started to recruit and introduce new training procedures to make the transformation easier when it comes. The soldiers in the Corps are pleased to be taking on a new role, rather than just being the Army's 'taxi service'.

Manpower and Training

The Army has been getting steadily smaller since the Second World War. This was mainly because of peace in Europe, but also due to a shrinking Empire. The Infantry, which has amalgamated to just under half its strength since the war, and the Armoured Corps, which has amalgamated all its regiments, now number only 12 per cent of the Army's total, compared with 36 per cent before the war. Most Infantry regiments have also been reduced to one or two battalions, the only notable exception being the Parachute Regiment, which remains at three, but the Parachute Regiment has never had problems filling their ranks until the increased resignations during 1994–5, which caused the MoD to draft in Gurkhas to fill the ranks.

The current manpower problems will be resolved over the coming years, and the likelihood of a reduction in those serving in Northern Ireland will lessen the burden faced by many regiments. Senior commanders predicted an up-turn in recruiting by the end of 1995, when the new advertisement campaign had taken hold and numbers leaving through the redundancy programme had levelled off. However, the prediction has so far failed to materialise and has been worsened by the increase in resignations, which was above expectations and far higher than those of the mid-1980s. In the period 1989–90, 20,400 men and 1,400 women joined the Army's ranks, yet in 1993–4 these figures had plummeted to 8,800 men and only 800 women. The outflow figures were also not encouraging, with 23,800 men and 1,300 women leaving during 1989–90 and 19,600 men and 1,300 women in 1993–4.

Even taking the redundancy programme into account, the figures leaving are far higher than the Army would like – so high, in fact, that the MoD is looking seriously at using both the Gurkhas and soldiers seconded from the Territorial Army. The Army's manpower figures are destined to drop to around 115,000 between late 1996 and 1997 and remain at that figure until 1999. This will help to steady the situation and remove the uncertainty many ranks are currently facing. But one problem that will not be so easy to solve is that of training facilities.

Brigade commanders are increasingly worried about the

reduction in exercise areas available to troops, especially in Germany, where the Soltau-Luneburg training area was closed in 1995. The need to keep Britain's commitment to the Allied Command Europe Rapid Reaction Force fully prepared for war must take precedence in future defence spending. Training grounds in the UK have come under extreme pressure in the last three years. With more troops requiring training and less space available, many regiments are having to use barracks for low-level training exercises. Although the military is looking for other suitable training areas both in the UK and abroad, it has no immediate solution to the problem.

What is likely to happen in the forthcoming years is more joint exercises with other armies, including non-Nato forces. In September 1994 the Coldstream Guards exercised in Hungary; in the same period the Scots Guards trained with the Polish armed forces at their Peace-Keeping Training Centre, and exercises with the Ukrainian and Romanian armies have also taken place. It has been decided that Denmark, Finland, Sweden and the UK will assist Estonia, Latvia and Lithuania to establish a joint military force, which paves the way for the possible establishment of training areas in the Baltic states.

The Army is also making full use of new computerised simulators, and advances in virtual reality have added a whole new dimension to infantry training. Not surprisingly, the Americans have been using computer-generated landscapes for some years, to test not only their helicopter pilots, but also their infantry and tank commanders.

While other military training areas have been reduced, the Army still uses the live-firing ranges in Canada to test battle groups in all aspects of combat, and this is the closest simulation of war available. Britain formally ended its operational commitment to Belize in mid-1994, but left behind a new British Army Training Support Unit; this 48-strong establishment will provide administrative support to visiting infantry battalions undergoing six weeks' jungle warfare training. There will be no permanent Army presence in this small state in the future, but training exercises will be completed.

Britain has always had strategic 'aircraft carriers' from which to mount world-wide operations; Ascension Island opens the southern hemisphere to such operations; Belize the Americas, and Cyprus the Middle East and the Gulf region.

Cyprus also has some of the best training areas available to the Army, with garrisons at Nicosia, Limassol and Larnaca able to provide accommodation and exercise terrain for visiting regiments from both the Regular and the Territorial Army. Unfortunately these areas are only for infantry units. The MoD will find new training areas but whether they will be adequate for the highly mobile and complex battle-group exercises of the future remains to be seen.

The Army as an Employer

The military is now seen as a good employer by many soldiers, although it fails to satisfy in terms of job security. Once the Army could guarantee a three-, six- or nine-year employment, but today soldiers are only safe for three years. The future, however, is sure to see a firm base being established for career soldiers to stay for the whole 22 years. The Army is sure to settle down into a period of reasonable stability after the last phase of redundancies is completed in 1996. This period will be spent redeploying troops to new areas, introducing computerised technology and advanced weaponry.

As technology advances and the Army integrates this equipment into front-line regiments, there is the chance that a new phase of reductions will be forced on it. For example, it has been suggested that infantrymen can be replaced by advanced sensors that will warn airborne attack helicopters of an impending attack. This would reduce the need for a large contingent of infantry or armoured soldiers on the battlefield. These advances can affect every area of the battlefield, to such an extent that fixed artillery pieces could be fired by remote control. Naturally, there will still be a need for soldiers but not in the numbers there are now.

The Soldiers

No matter what changes are made, the British soldier has always been able to adapt. The ending of conscription and the later amalgamations of the 1960s did not breed a new soldier, and nor has the radical reorganisation of the 1990s. The soldiers that make up the majority of the Army's manpower, no matter what the generation, have always been special, and they will always remain special. What many civilians fail to understand is that all soldiers, whether men or women, are prepared to die for their country. They have given up the right to make their own decisions or choose their own paths to glory, and although many soldiers would not admit it, they all crave war, crave the opportunity to fight for their country, not, as many seem to think, because they have a killing instinct, but because they want to be respected and remembered for their determination, bravery and courage.

Today, war veterans look back to the Second World War and the Falklands Campaign and remember comrades who fell in the line of duty, killed for what they honestly believed was right, defending this country. No matter where in the world British soldiers are sent to fight, they will fight with the same determination, guts and bravado that have made them one of the most fierce fighting forces in the world. No politician could ever change that.

Select Bibliography

Although most of the research for this book was conducted through personal interviews, I have made use of facts, figures and historical information from the annual statements on defence, the regular publications of the House of Commons Select Committee on Defence and the National Audit Office Reports on the Drawdown of Equipment and Stores. In addition, I have made use of the following books:

Beevor, Anthony, *Inside the British Army*, Chatto & Windus Ltd (1991)

Carver, Michael, *Tightrope Walking* (1992)

Dillion, G.M. (ed), *Defence Policy Making: A Comparative Analysis* (1988)

Geraghty, Tony, *Who Dares Wins*, Little, Brown & Co (1992)

Greenwood, David, *Reshaping Nato's Defences* (1990)

Griffen, David, *British Army Regiments*, Patrick Stephens Ltd (1985)

Kennedy, Paul, *The Rise and Fall of the Great Powers*, Unwin Hyman (1988)

Mileham, P.J., *The Scottish Regiments*, Spellmount (1988).

Simpkin Richard, *Race to the Swift*, Brassey's (1985)

Urban, Mark, *Big Boys Rules*, Faber & Faber (1992)

Glossary of
Army Jargon and Slang

Back-squadded To be moved back one squad during training.

Badged After successfully passing selection for the Special Air Service troopers are 'badged'. Could also mean a member of a regiment.

Beasting Intense physical training or drill during training sessions. Could also imply bullying by NCOs.

Bimble To walk without hurry. Used generally to imply slowness.

Bin To get rid of something. Recruits can also be 'binned', meaning to be removed from training.

Birdshit Nickname for soldiers serving within the Parachute Regiment.

Bivvy Abbreviation for a bivouac shelter. Made from an Army one-man tent or using natural material from the surrounding area.

Blade-runner An ambitious Sandhurst cadet determined to win the Sword of Honour.

Blanket-stacker Member of the Royal Logistics Corps or soldiers working in regimental quartermaster stores.

Bleeps Members of the Royal Signals, also called 'scaley-backs'.

Blue-on-blue Clash between friendly forces during combat or live-firing exercises.

Bluey Forces aerogramme letter.

Bog standard Basic or common.

Brown-nose Soldiers who agree to any task or volunteer for fatigues given by officers.

Budgies Nickname for Fusiliers because of the hackle worn on their beret capbadge.

Bust To be demoted or stripped of rank.

Cam-up To camouflage a vehicle or position.

Chuff-chart Used by soldiers to tick off the days to do during exercises or postings.

Chunkies Members of the Royal Pioneer Corps.

Death by vu-foil Instruction within a classroom.

Desert-speak Gulf jargon.

Dhobi   Laundry or washing.

Dicked   To be put on a bad job or fatigue.

Dicker   An IRA member watching British troops or a spotter for a remote-control explosion.

Diffy   Lacking equipment through loss or theft, to be deficient.

Dockyard confetti   Home-made terrorist bomb using nuts and bolts or ball-bearings as shrapnel.

Dropshort   A member of the Royal Artillery.

Dummy run   A rehearsal of a military exercise.

Egyptian PT   Sleeping during the day, normally done on sports afternoons.

Endex   The end of an exercise.

FIN   Fin-stabilizing discarding sabot. A tank round that is capable of penetrating armour up to 3 inches thick.

FINCO   Field intelligence NCO from the Intelligence Corps. Could be an agent-handler or someone who operates undercover.

Friendly fire   See 'Blue-on-blue'.

Fudge factor   Manipulation of manpower statistics.

Gash   Anything or anybody considered useless.

Gimpy   A general-purpose machine-gun.

Gonk   To sleep.

Gopping   Disgusting.

Grab-a-granny night   A weekly event among single soldiers to see who can attract and sleep with the oldest, and more often than not the ugliest, woman in a bar or night-club.

Green Army   The uniformed Army in Northern Ireland.

Grot   A man who is untidy or refuses to wash.

Grunt   An Infantry soldier.

Heavy army   Armoured divisions as opposed to the 'light army' of the Infantry.

Jack   A soldier who works alone. Also known as 'on his Jack Jones'.

Jack it in   To give up.

Leg it   To run away.

Lemoned   To be given a bad job. Sometimes referred to as 'jiffed', depending on the regiment.

Lift   To arrest a suspect in Northern Ireland.

Liney   A Royal Signals linesman.

Loggies   Members of the Logistics Corps.

Lose your teddy   To become angry or upset. Can also mean to leave the Army in a huff.

Lurker   A coward or skiver.

Maggot   Army-issue green sleeping bag.

Mark one eyeball   Using the naked eye rather than optical equipment.

Mattress-back   Someone who spends all his spare time in bed. Can also mean a loose girl.

Milling   Military boxing used by the Paratroopers to develop aggression.

Mod plod   A Ministry of Defence policeman.

Monkey   A military policeman.

Naafi   Navy Army Air Force Institutes. The organisation which operates service shops and canteens in barracks.

Opsi   Operator in Special Intelligence. An Intelligence Corps specialist trade.

Orbat   Order of battle. The official organisation of the field army.

Out-of-area   Outside the NATO region like the Falklands or Cyprus.

Pads   Married men, short for 'married pad', as opposed to 'singlies'.

Paddy-bashing   Service in Northern Ireland with the possibility of 'lifting' an IRA suspect.

Pan-bashing   Cookhouse fatigue, washing-up.

Pit   A bed.

Plank   A Royal Artillery gunner: from the First World War, when the dead bodies of gun crews were put under the wheels to stop the gun from sinking into the mud.

Ponti   Person with no real tactical purpose.

Push out the zeds   To sleep.

Rodney or Rupert   An Army officer.

Scaley-backs   Members of the Royal Signals Corps.

Schoolies   Young girls from service schools who chase soldiers. (Also a derogatory term for RAEC or AGC (ETS) officers?)

Schrank Syndrome   When Germany-based soldiers and their wives buy large wall units on credit to replace Army-issue furniture.

Scoff or scran   To eat.

Shreddies   Underpants. Could also be called 'skiddies'.

Shufti   To take a look at something.

Singlies   Unmarried soldiers.

Skive   To escape from a duty. Can also mean a great way to swan off.

Slop jockey   An Army Catering Corps cook.

Slot   To kill someone.

Smoker   A drinking session, normally held round a fire while on exercise. This has since been ruled out in Germany after complaints from civilians about the damage to local woods caused by soldiers.

Sneaky-beaky   Covert intelligence operations.

Stag   Normally a two-hour sentry duty.

Tab To march cross country, or to 'yomp'.

Track-bashing Routine maintenance work on armoured vehicles.

Trogs Members of the Royal Armoured Corps.

Whinger A man who constantly complains.

Yellow handbag A pack of ten Herford Biers carried by soldiers in Germany. Also known as a 'ten pack'.

Zulu warrior Activity in which a soldier strips off to music while other drunken soldiers chant and sing 'The zulu warrior' and then cover him in beer.

Conventional Forces in Europe (CFE) Treaty

The CFE treaty, ratified in November 1990, imposed limits on tanks, armoured personnel vehicles, aircraft and helicopters in the central European theatre.

The figures are:

	Western	Eastern
Tanks:	20,000	13,300
Artillery:	20,000	13,700
APC:	30,000	20,000
Aircraft:	6,800	5,150
Helicopters:	2,000	1,500

Although these figures were maximums, no power except the Soviet Union could come close to them. Britain's declared figures for 1990 and 1996 are:

	1990	1996
Tanks:	1,198	1,015
Artillery:	636	636
APC:	3,193	N/A
Aircraft:	842	900
Helicopters:	368	384

Height to
Weight Ratio Table

All potential recruits should have the correct height to weight ratio. Below is a guide to help applicants identify their correct ratio. So if your height is 5ft 4in then your weight should be around 9st 6lb for a man and 9st for a woman.

MEN				WOMEN	
(St.lb)	**(Kg)**	**(Ft.in)**	**(m)**	**(St.lb)**	**(kg)**
8.13	56.7	5.2	1.57	8.6	53.5
9.2	58.1	5.3	1.60	8.10	55.3
9.6	59.9	5.4	1.63	9.0	57.2
9.10	61.7	5.5	1.65	9.4	59.0
10.0	63.5	5.6	1.68	9.8	60.8
10.4	65.3	5.7	1.70	9.12	62.6
10.8	67.1	5.8	1.73	10.2	64.4
10.13	69.4	5.9	1.75	10.7	66.7
11.4	71.7	5.10	1.78	10.12	68.9
11.9	73.9	5.11	1.80	11.3	71.2
12.0	76.2	6.0	1.83	11.8	73.5
12.5	78.5	6.1	1.85	11.12	75.3
12.10	80.7	6.2	1.88	12.4	78.0

British Army Officer Ranks and Appointments Structure

Field Marshal: Chief of the Defence Staff

General: Chief of the General Staff or Commander-in-Chief

Lieutenant-General: Corps Commander

Major-General: Divisional Commander

Brigadier: Brigade Commander

Colonel: Senior Staff Appointment

Lieutenant-Colonel: Commanding Officer of a Battalion or Regiment

Major: Company or Squadron Commander

Captain: Regimental Adjutant or Second-in-Command of a Company or Squadron

Lieutenant or 2nd Lieutenant: Platoon or Troop Commander

British Army NCO Ranks and Appointments Structure

Regimental Sergeant-Major
(Warrant Officer Class I)

Company/Squadron/Battery
Sergeant-Major
(Warrant Officer Class II)

Colour/Staff Sergeant

Sergeant

Corporal/Bombardier

Lance Corporal/Lance Bombardier

Private / Trooper / Gunner / Signalman
Guardsman / Fusilier / Ranger / Rifleman / Kingsman
Craftsman / Sapper / Driver / Air Trooper

The Household Division has variations. Sergeant-majors are called corporal-majors and sergeants are called corporals of horse. Foot Guard corporals are referred to as lance-sergeants and all Foot Guard NCOs wear one extra stripe.

Index

Index

Index